What people are say

Baba Yaga - Slavic Ea

I've felt for a long time that there must be more in the call to Baba Yaga's cottage than the fairy tales tell us. Natalia Clarke has drawn on her Siberian heritage and personal insights in this powerful piece to show us how we might approach this powerful Goddess. This is a book for anyone drawn to dark Goddesses and Crone Goddesses. It's also the first map I've seen that explores the forests in search of wild Gods who will not make themselves comfortable in our homes or on our altars. It's ground-breaking stuff.

Nimue Brown

A truly fascinating book that opens up our understanding and knowledge of this perhaps misunderstood Goddess. Natalia Clarke shares personal experiences mixed with folklore and practical information to guide seekers to find their own connection with Baba Yaga.

Rachel Patterson

This is an impressive work, clearly written, exploring Baba Yaga as Earth Goddess and laying out what an apprenticeship with her might look like. In a culture that tends to categorise everything - emotions, actions, people - as either wholly good or wholly bad, this book brings some much needed nuance and an exploration of a healthy darkness through this fantastic, visceral deity.

Meredith Debonnaire

Pagan Portals

Baba Yaga
Slavic Earth Goddess

Pagan Portals
Baba Yaga
Slavic Earth Goddess

Natalia Clarke

**MOON
BOOKS**

Winchester, UK
Washington, USA

JOHN HUNT PUBLISHING

First published by Moon Books, 2021
Moon Books is an imprint of John Hunt Publishing Ltd., No. 3 East Street, Alresford
Hampshire SO24 9EE, UK
office@jhpbooks.net
www.johnhuntpublishing.com
www.moon-books.net

For distributor details and how to order please visit the 'Ordering' section on our website.

Text copyright: Natalia Clarke 2020

ISBN: 978 1 78904 878 0
978 1 78904 879 7 (ebook)
Library of Congress Control Number: 2020951017

A CIP catalogue record for this book is available from the British Library.

Design: Stuart Davies

UK: Printed and bound by CPI Group (UK) Ltd, Croydon, CR0 4YY
Printed in North America by CPI GPS partners

We operate a distinctive and ethical publishing philosophy in
all areas of our business, from our global network of authors to
production and worldwide distribution.

Contents

To know her is to know nature
To know nature is to know yourself

Deep in the birch forest she dwells between the human and non-human worlds. With every rising sun she witnesses the darkness and light in nature and the world. She doesn't participate, but joins its unfolding in quiet observation. Nothing surprises or moves her. She's seen it all since the time began. It is the cycle of repeat that she frowns upon from where humans dwell, although cycles in nature sustain her. She holds the balance between the good and bad, dark and light, wet and dry, rich and barren. Maintaining it is feeding herself as they are one and whole.

Her hut is her womb, her food is her cells both human and non-human, her oven is her cauldron and all the animals about her are kin. In secure privacy she wants for nothing and when she cares she decides what for. She ventures out in her mortar or as a bird she grows wings and flies all over the Earth rejoicing in her all-knowing, and in that she's content: free and at home in her being.

She smells the human which repulses her to the core yet amidst the stench she detects a scent of the primal, just born, wilderness lost in someone out there crying to come out. Her face flashes and she changes form from a child to a young girl, to a mother holding a babe, to an old hag. The house begins to dance in chaos jingling pans and pots inside it and bones about her dwelling join in with an ear-piercing rattle. The Three Horsemen stand together at the ready, side by side.

She's called. Will she go? She turns into a raven and flies to oversee. She hears the deep cry within a human that will either meet their death or salvation at her wisdom. She must decide. She will either kill or save it. It will either be safe out of its womb or it will die not knowing.

Facing the demise of what's familiar and precious and becoming wild again is the quest of brave and raw ones. Are you one?

Introduction

This is a story of a Crone like no other you've heard or read about before. It is a re-defining of an archetypal folk figure that for time immemorial has been portrayed in certain ways through culture, history and literature. She's more than a wicked witch of the forest that devours children and scares all that is human and makes us run from all that is dark. She's been exiled from society and made into a hateful murderer one should avoid at all cost. To me she is an Earth Goddess. Will she share her wisdom with those of us prepared to be taught? Can we throw away the clothes of deceit and misconceptions about her and about ourselves? Can we be brave enough to be stripped to the bone, to the very essence that had been buried within us all for far too long? None of us have escaped and got to keep the skin we came into the world with. We have all been stripped bare in the face of culture, society, war and politics. Some shed more skins than others. Many seek its reclamation actively, others have given up and given in, and many will never realise it has been lost long ago. The question is "what about you?" Do you feel the deep yearning and the need to reclaim yourself? This is a story for the brave and vulnerable, for the pioneers of self-discovery in a different way.

First of all, I would like to offer you a brief traditional description of Baba Yaga, as a folklore figure from Slavic culture, traditions and mythology. The figure has featured in children's stories and fairy tales as an old hag, who lives in the woods, for hundreds of years. She is portrayed as a terrifying entity, someone to fear greatly with an appetite for children. She is old and wild with white messy hair and a crooked nose featuring a large wart. Her nails are long and hard like an animal's claws, and she has many helpers such as her magical house on chicken legs, her flying mortar and broom and the gates, doors and locks

1

in the shape of human remains with skulls featuring strongly around her dwelling in a clearing in thick woods. There are animals around, who assist her and the Three Horsemen. She is believed to eat enough food for ten people and to resent all things human. The word "Baba" in Russian means 'a woman old enough to marry'. The story of Baba Yaga and Vasilisa the Wise is one of the most well-known tales, and provides an underlying thread for my inspiration and exploration of what it means to know yourself.

When embarking on this project I was asked what this book was to be about. Was it going to be another fairy tale? A short-story collection? Poetry? A description of the character popularised in literature and TV programmes in Slavic culture? A caricature of a grotesque figure created to be used as a scare figure for children and a mystery to humans?

This book is a snapshot of my relationship with the deity/ archetype/energy/Earth spirit in a psycho-spiritual sense where I attempt to answer a few questions about what Baba Yaga is and isn't from my perspective of relating to her; what her main lessons are and how, if willing, one can integrate the qualities and wisdom of this Earth Goddess; into your own spiritual practice and your life in general.

I am an intuitive person and my life is based on intuitive knowing whatever I embark on. My magic practice is also intuitive and when Baba Yaga came forward one day and said she wanted to be talked about, I had to listen. In truth I had been waiting for an invitation for many years and there it finally was. Ideas, observations and explorations in this book are based on my own experience and understanding of this Goddess. Interpreting the symbols and stories associated with her have come to me through listening deeply and going into her essence, be it through her whisperings in the night or dreams or actively learning and relating to the ideas and concepts that she exists by. One thing was for certain, I knew that I needed to write her story down essentially, as it was unfolding in me and in front of me through her presence and energy. After many years of seeking and waiting she was near, showing herself and beginning to speak.

My aim with this introductory guide of working with a deity is to spark curiosity about Baba Yaga. I describe how she comes to me and what her world, concepts, presentations and ideas mean to me, my magic practice and my self-development. How, via my responses and engagement with her work, my life is affected. Why my relationship with her is useful, creative and meaningful to me and in what areas.

I touch upon her place within an Earth-based spirituality and explore the meaning of her qualities and behaviours in that context rather than in literary, cultural or societal concepts and beliefs. My personal relationship with her is based on how I understand her, and how she comes to manifest in my reality. Each of us will have some similar and some very different experiences as we are not all alike, but there are some common characteristics we all share. She is what she is and can be chaotic, the rule is not to fit or force or fix her in any particular place or practice. This is what culture, literature and history have done and here I am breaking away from that and seeking to present her as she is. That is the key. Who is she without any of the prescribed characteristics? I intend to present this through my journey with her so far.

I would like to offer an example of a Goddess with much bigger ideas than first meets the eye. I offer interpretations of how she can be incorporated into your spiritual practice and your life and what her value is to the world. I would like to inspire you to look at her, and maybe other deities, as beings with whom you can form a relationship, a collaboration, a sacred union towards balance. I hope to bring enthusiasm and inspiration into the work with subjects that interest you like Baba Yaga has always interested me; an interest, which brought questions, and a wondering curiosity to look beyond the persona of a fairy tale.

I invite you on a journey of being with her and experiencing the journey into her realms via your own magic. I aim to portray and share my story of a relationship with her with grace, intimacy and respect. I invite you to draw your own lessons from her if you decide to work with or are called upon by her.

In 2020 Baba Yaga did not feel like returning to the underworld for spring and summer, but decided to hang around for a bit longer, as she, herself was curious about the reactions in the world and the dramatic unfolding of collective shadow. Writing this book during 2020 is not a coincidence. She whispered to me during the winter and I heard her. Little did I know of the reason or understand the timing of this, but luckily, I tend to follow my intuition without questioning the motives. With intuition something like this brings an instant insight: the voices that speak through it are clear as day and I need nothing else. As the journey unfolded this year, I saw the reason, I heard the motivation and I embraced the purpose of this work; as it was asking to be propelled into the world and into human consciousness. This time is full of personal and collective tragedy, a deep yearning for expression and personal empowerment. It is time when using our voices is not just necessary: it is unquestionably life-saving if we are to move towards healing on a wider scale. We can no longer stay still, silent and in the shadows. She stayed with me this year till the end of May and then quietly slipped away into her domain giving space to the Maiden hoping that this time she is sufficiently armed with wanting to speak the message on behalf of the Crone. This is unusual, but these times are not what we have encountered before, so one might say she stepped up to the plate. I heard her, saw her and committed to the work.

In this book I would like most of all to give Baba Yaga a voice. What is she as herself when she's not upholding a role in a particular story and not relating to yet another hero? Who is she as herself? She's been enslaved, manipulated and misunderstood. Depending on the message and motivations of the hero she's portrayed as either good or evil, but what is it that she wants to be? What is it that she is? I am interested in looking at, and relating to her from outside the fairy tale persona and as the Goddess that she is to me. When she's set free and observed in freedom, allowed to function how she does and invited into kinship, what will she then be and what will she choose to do?

Chapter 1

Who is Baba Yaga Really?

Historically, her name is associated with negative emotions, scary vibrations that are meant not to attract, but repel, reflected in the translations of her name below. She is not an example of who to be or how to live a life. Her name means:

'Horror and shudder' in Serbian and Croatian.
'Anger' in Slovenian.
'Wicked wood nymph' in modern Czech.
'Fury' in Polish.
She is the Dark Goddess, traditionally coming from the Slavic
    cultures of Eastern Europe.
The huntress.
The dryad.
The forest spirit.
The shapeshifter.
No stranger to blood bones and gore.
Territorial, like an animal, hence her protective homestead.
Deity.
Energy.
Witch.
The wise woman.
Supernatural figure.
Folklore legend.
The ruler of the Elements.
The bone mother.
Raw nature spirit.
Mother Archetype.
A psycho-spiritual guide.
The queen of the underworld, the old Persephone, who

knows it all.
The Triple Goddess.
Animal speaker.
Spirit of the dead.
Queen of afterlife.
Embodied seasons.
Dweller of multidimensional realities.
Elder.
Wise-self.
The Universe.

When you look at her face; close up, terrifying yet knowing beyond anything imaginable, you don't only see yourself, you see the whole world, continents, mountain ranges, oceans, the burning Sun and the fullest silver bright Moon. She is the Earth itself. To me she is a true Earth Goddess.

She is complex, yet values simplicity of life and sight. She believes in using herself and only herself whatever the challenge. She assists others only when she is willing. It is the prep-work that is big and challenging for anyone seeking a path of wisdom, satisfaction and life-fulfilment. To encounter her is to transform and those, who are ready to listen, observe, work hard and persevere will receive her assistance... perhaps...

It you stumble upon her unaware or unprepared or "young" in your consciousness, your fate will be uncertain and if you manage to find your way back from the dark woods you will be confused and unsettled. Before she agrees to apprentice you into the work of transformation, she requires clarity of thought and sight, a sharpness of all senses and an ability to see through and beyond the veils of the world and into the spiritual realm. She is wise beyond measure and will only respect commitment to knowledge. She will smell your fear, your lack of determination, but she will also know when courage and a desire to learn burns bright within you. She also responds to kindness – a rarity in her world, something that, perhaps, speaks of the wounds of human existence in her or a representation of withdrawing from society.

Children-eating associations stem from an old tale and a technique of scaring children into submission, as if fear is the best tool. We all know that when we are scared, we cling to our mothers and it makes for a union, although not a very authentic one. Children are not trusted with their imagination or to dwell in the dark. Perhaps, she sees children as the possessions of adults; unreachable just like their parents, and she devours the qualities she deems useless: innocence and the lack of will and direction.

One has to be in a certain position/stage of psychic and spiritual development to be able to truly hear her teachings and become a learner of her magic. She requires sacrifice and takes no prisoners. So, you'd better be sure. If you like a challenge, she is the one for you. Journeying with her requires care and attention at all times and most of all she demands respect. She has a temper and it is easy for her to use it. She is fearless. If there is no engagement she will simply disappear and disengage. Will you get the second chance? Only you know. Will she be there again? Only she decides.

Her ambivalent/contradictory presentation holds a key to the representation of the whole, which I welcome. She might be seen as cruel, wicked, uncaring and terrifying. She knows what evil is, but she also holds an overwhelming desire for kindness and does not tolerate cruelty of any kind. In recent years, Baba Yaga's desire for kindness has been a large part of my experience of her and I consciously addressed my own quality of kindness and its meaning. The collective unconscious holds evil and divine as being in opposition; it is polarised. Thus, things are either blessed or cursed depending on what goal there is to be achieved. Both can be manipulated, and used in service to any society that rules through division, guilt and shame. The idea of wholeness, of being both light and dark, is seen as nonsensical and useless, even dangerous. Polarisation is a form of control after all.

To me it is evident that it is kindness that she responds to despite popular opinions and representations. It is the beauty underneath the scarred body that she represents; it is the life in the depth of hellish experiences, and she calls for resurrection. She is the one, who showed me on a much deeper level what kindness can do. She reprimands with a piercing stare or a loud sound when I forget. She always brings the mirror right up to my face. Over time, I am becoming uninterested in anything but kindness through the restoration of the heart.

Dark night, thick forest and cold wind. Three knights on horseback guarding her territory: one white, one red and one black. They represent dawn, midday and night. A clearing in the forest, a wooden hut on chicken legs surrounded by a fence made of human bones with skulls on top. The gates are human legs, the locks are human hands and sharp teeth. The eyes in the skulls are lit up and the clearing filled with light like daytime. The Earth begins to shake underfoot, she is flying in her mortar with a broom sweeping up behind her. She can smell human and it fills her with disgust. It is hard to escape the place due to her helpers in the forms of trees and animals and only with her words can the gates open and close. "Hut, hut, turn your back to the woods and front towards me."

I have also been conditioned into valuing the light and fearing the dark. I complied, as mother said, until personal darkness descended on me and traumatic experiences permeated my life. I was not prepared, and I fell apart. Darkness pulled me under, gripping my being at its core. In the dark, drowning, I learnt slowly what darkness and light truly meant.

She said "The world needs me." My heart expanded with my reverence for her understanding and acceptance. Collective darkness has been rising to uncontainable levels. It has been permeating through every area of our lives for a long time in floods, in bloody violence, in the exploitation and silencing of the wise voice. The world turned away from darkness, and in doing so projected everything ugly onto something "other": nature, each other, the rest of the world. Anywhere but within.

Her idea of darkness is different. Her greatest value is placed in the darkness of the Earth as a potential for growth and transformation. She calls towards the journey down with an intention of rising up. She invites those, who have outlived conditioning and outgrown their tight moulding, who have survived the dark manifestation of projections, who have stared fear in the face on many occasions and kept going, who see gold in the darkest depths of consciousness and are willing to take the journey through the dark woods. She gathers them in. She speaks of how to get out of the woods, one needs to go in as deep as possible. Venom drips from her rotten teeth as she picks them out with her claw-like nails and as it drops on the Earth trees begin to grow, because that is always her intention, to turn matter into spirit and dark into light, and death into life. A skull with a fire inside it, in the hands of a conscious person, is a holy grail, a well of infinite potential.

Her idea of the darkness is a rich domain of gifts and unique qualities that have been rejected and have lain dormant there for a long time. It is our job to rediscover them. They will be what lets us see the light again.

We might want to ponder what the consequences are of just being darkness or just being light? There has to be a balance and Baba Yaga recognises that more than anyone ever could. She was born into both darkness and light and, yes, labels got attached to her due to cultural adaptations and religious necessities, but the essence of her, and every one of us, has remained the same. Balance is what she is all about and she seeks to know how balanced we are. It is one of the questions she will ask when someone shows willingness to apprentice into her magic (more on that later).

She is the Grandmother of balance. She is of the darkest night in Siberian mid-winter when all you can see is the low sky where every star is a face, a voice, a message from the world. She is of the brightest, most tender light in the spring birch forest where she takes off her hair covering and lets her silver hair sway in the wind of change before she has to retreat, giving way to a new cycle. She reshapes and shifts into brooks and awakening tree leaves; into a bear coming out of its hide into a new season; into birds busying themselves with creating families. She grieves for winter, for her darkness that is her most comfortable home, for the fire that warms her hut and cooks her food. She adapts, she knows the way. She has to wait, to sing in the silence of her retreat till the next traveller comes knocking. She is of snow and bones, white on the outside and hollow inside in a state of collapse without covering, armour or protection.

Her image and persona contains a large number of symbols, associations and traits that might or might not appeal. Remaining curious is a good way forward. Let your imagination, intuition, self-awareness and wonder lead you to what you can work with. Do not rush or you will get overwhelmed and confused by what's needed and what's being thrown into the mix to trick or muddle you. We are dealing with a playful trickster here, someone that does not reveal. She can point or hint but never tells the whole story otherwise what teacher she would be if she revealed all the answers? It is a quest, a challenge that she works with and admires the trier, the patient and committed. It is in the apprenticeship that she finds fun and enjoyment. She needs to know how willing and ready you are to really step into the unknown. She does not hold or protect or guide. She sees. She will ask if you know *who you are and what you are for* – the most important questions of all. What do you want? She has no interest in your fear or in you. She is interested in what you are made of and whether you know it or not. Are you even willing to find out? She tests your will and your ability to discern between paths. She provokes and treats you with scepticism and doubt just to see if it affects you. She's indifferent in many way, neutral and that's what Earth is.

She's interested in the original story, script, primal material. Who were you before you went into the world? We go back to her to be reminded of the primal materials, which we came here with before life happened.

She eats children: why? They are the original primal matter, the Source: clean and pure, unspoilt and nourishing. They surrender without fear. In human reality, as we know it, children are scared by her and she is not interested in those who are scared. By the time kids understand the stories they have been changed and manipulated with the script that life gives us. We all hear the same messages and we have no choice but to take it on as truth otherwise how do we fit in? Power is taken away, and the fight against soul begins. What does she say about soul? Her language is of the matter that is Earth, Water, Air and Fire. The soul essence is a life force that wants to be and to thrive towards expression. That is the language of Baba Yaga.

It is a language that is never in doubt and always expressing itself through the seasons, Elements and cycles. It is simple in its certainty of life and existence. To her this is soul. We, however, continue fighting against it, we look in places that have long forgotten that link and its importance as part of ourselves.

Often curious heroes on a journey come to her, but they don't know why they do what they do. It's always about conquering evil, defeating a beast or gaining respect or winning a Maiden. As if a Maiden wants to be won and a beast is in some way inferior to the hero. What is the respect of those that only tell one story and live by one truth, which is narrated over and over again with no change for generations? She is bored after an eternity of hearing the same story; the same hero looking for the same challenges that are pre-made and devoid of creativity. She craves the story to be re-written through us, to have a hero like no other before, who does not robotically follow what "others" have said he should do and go where he's told to go. Often there isn't even a map or an invitation to self-create on a traditional journey. The hero works it out with the help of many and we, in life, work it out too, but does he even want to do whatever it is he started? Do we? Does he actually care or is the preconception of who he needs to be so deeply programmed that he must be the same as those that came before him. This is where "going off the path" (more on that later) is important. Following a path where there are no breadcrumbs, going to places where no human has stepped before. Baba Yaga's teachings are to be explorative, daring, creative, and curious and yes, one might be scared, but when one is willing to look for things beyond that fear something new and different happens. The old pattern is broken. Daring to be different might be for nothing and you might have to turn back and join the familiar trodden path, but by taking that detour in the first place energy will have been changed and, your body will have locked it in, that exciting feeling of the unknown. You will have gotten in touch with your primal self, the one that wanted to return to the original story that has been untold for all eternity that has remained hidden amidst the darkest woods until you dared to reclaim it, to walk to the heart of the matter, the clearing in the deep dark forest.

She often says "you don't know you are born" and she laughs in a reproaching way, yes, in an unforgiving way, yes. She turns the mirror on us so we can see exactly how it is that we are being with and to ourselves in life while struggling through it.

"What are you for? Why are you here? Those are questions I hear from her more and more often.

She asks what you want your story to be. She is not interested in what it has been: she knows. She will only express some interest, in her unique way, if she sees that you are asking different questions and life no longer answers and you feel it:

the presence of Baba Yaga.

She doesn't like company for long. The window is narrow and her time is never wasted, so the questions you come to her with have to be the right questions and your language and manner has to be those that please her: if she likes what she hears she might grant a day or two of her fleeting company which amounts to some hours only as her main duties of guarding life and communing with nature takes priority. She's set in her duties and habits and in the flow of all things natural. She's not distracted.

In the autumn, when my magic is most alive, she's there patting me on the back; if she feels like it, and enjoying witnessing alignment and magic in someone else. At other times of the year she's busy and quiet and often unreachable. She's not someone to summon, and she doesn't summon you as she has no interest in anything in the human reality. She walks the edges of the veils and shows herself at changing seasons. This makes her unique, but also makes her the most Earth-like Goddess as the Earth continues unmoved by us, and so does she.

She doesn't feel like a grandmother or an old Crone with terrifying features. She's a master shapeshifter, and her essence is that of nature itself. She's the changing seasons, the leaves in the forest in autumn and a smell of the coming snow storm. She's footsteps on the ice and a cold mountain brook. She is like the wind as she flies and in the whooshing sound of a breeze she's gone. She's the smoke in the dark and she can be found in animal bones. She is in the smallest insect and the highest tree, the snake hiding in the undergrowth. Illusive, unobtrusive, hardly ever visible and fiercely private. Her dwelling is her own and, on her terms, where everything is just so. It is for no one else to make sense of.

The poem below was written post-lockdown in 2020 and inspired by the idea of asking the right questions; the big questions:

What am I for?

A bird, a tree, a rock; they know what they are for, what freedom is.

Simplicity of it pierces through me breaking my heart for I can't reach that state of knowing.

Human...

I am misplaced, shapeshifted here and there, but nowhere I know what I am for.

I do it all and do it well, as there's nothing else to be done.

Yet there is always a bodily grumble, a jerk and a sting in the tongue, as all joy is lost or never there.

What am I for? I do not know.

In constant searching I tire, desiring for extinction, yet if not searching then what?

Grabbing onto something, anything, somewhere, but nothing stays as it should, or should it not be that way?

Is being misplaced a 'what for' in itself?

The non-human calls me, as it knows what is what.

It has always known and for that I love it so.

Thrown into this life one more time I swam and walked straight off with confidence, but devoid of knowing what I was for.

Was I for something, but no more? Seem to have had and lost too early, known too soon, aged ahead of time.

Is that it? Neither a witch nor a monk, but both.

I seem to know a lot of parts.

A bit of everything, but no one thing and I want to be that one thing.

Past love returns through dreams to remind me of the loss and the feeling that burns with such purity and light.

It hurts, but the pain is sweet, the pain is deadly, yet alive.

Is love what I was for, but no longer?

I drop it all now and again, empty out to make a way for something to take shape, to become once more.

It comes, it stays, and it fuels, but not for long before the craving rises up again for "What am I for?"

Now and again I grab hold of the golden thread and cherish it for a time before it slips out of my hand once again to become something or anything, but not mine.

Am I a shapeshifting entity adapting to what is? Is that enough? Is that worthy of staying, being?

Perhaps it's always been nothing solid or constant

Perhaps it is in the flow. I speak of the flow often.

Why doesn't yearning stop and why does bitterness grow at times?

Why does the peace elude me and tears always stand on ready?

Perhaps, it is a part of a crying body; dark texture of a human that also wants to be.

And I am a carrier of its skin and depth.

Perhaps, that is just so and what if that is not me, or one or constant.

Perhaps, I am the ever-changing sketch of all things life, all voices of the unknown.

In times of tiredness I crave the knowledge of the way of trees, rocks and birds.

It comes over and over, but a shapeshifter needs rest, space, and formlessness, hence emptiness is a necessary part of life too.

What am I for?

A lifetime spent asking questions is a life worth having

Perhaps...

Chapter 2

My Story

My childhood ended at five years of age when my "good mother" left me. I now know she had to, as I was a restless infant, toddler and then child, always looking for more and seeing further, never content and always in my feelings. Challenges followed me from birth and I revelled in overcoming them. My mother felt she was no longer enough or needed, as I became fiercely independent and moved away from her. I was not a child she could be with in a way that she knew how to. In the physical sense she remained, but in every other sense we separated. I needed to find another mother, "a mature one", "a wise one" and I attached to my grandmother. The energy of her wisdom felt like a comfortable skin on my body and I absorbed stories, magic, card readings and so much more. I could read, write and do mathematics by the time I reached five. I was ready for the world, but the world wasn't ready for me, so struggles continued on my way to freedom and to finding my own wise woman, an inner mother who is neither rejecting nor smothering. One thing I knew I could not be controlled or moulded.

Baba Yaga was present since the times I was tiny when my father read me fairy tales every night. I learnt them all by heart. Instead of fear for her I felt fascination and curiosity and my parents knew instinctively that scaring me with her would never work. I always laughed at her appearance in wonder and wished I could meet her. She was different and quirky, like me. I didn't fit in and fiercely resisted every attempt at shaping me that came from the outside. I think I also searched for Baba Yaga. My passion for the forest was also born with me; it was there even before I knew that I knew it. Being in the forest with birds, insects and trees was like Heaven on Earth and I am grateful to my family for being in tune with that part of me, as they had it running through their blood too – a love for nature, as our one true home and mother.

When I was about ten years old, I fell mysteriously ill and was healed by a witch, a very old woman from a small village located in the Ural mountain region of the Siberian plain. She felt powerful all over and her presence demanded complete concentration, co-operation and respect from everyone in the house. Her healing was to happen on her terms whatever it took. She was petite, short, with the kindest face I had ever seen and a voice that went from deep and booming to the highest pitch possible, as sweet as a bird-song in spring. I was fascinated and surrendered to her spell instantly. I remember that experience vividly and to this day I know the feeling of being touched by magic. That old lady was magic. It is said that some powers can be passed on from one person to another if at the time of a ritual or a healing ceremony the other is open and receptive. Often the time when these transferred powers or elements of them come into awareness and manifestation is not till much later in a woman's life; not till cronehood commences.

That day I felt changed and, yes, I was healed from an ailment that no doctor could explain. I also remember my mother asking the witch to cure my constant crying along with the mysterious disease I was afflicted with. I cried a lot and I cried openly. The woman said to my mother, "She will need her tears". Do you hear the message in that? She knew getting rid of an emotional expression would not serve me or anyone. My mother asked for it, as she was not able to bear my pain or my fear. I continued to cry and for that I am grateful. I have valued emotions highly ever since, as the best messengers from within us, my most valuable navigational system. The wisdom of the emotional and intuitive states is for a woman a priceless gift of the witch. Those are her allies in knowing how to know, be, act and respond. At that time, she passed something on to me.

The house later burnt down to the ground and with it my grandmother's whole homestead including the trees, all the animals, the garden, vegetable plot and all the outbuildings. My maternal grandmother never recovered from the blow and died of a stroke soon after. The only thing that was left standing in the smouldering ashes after the fire settled was a post from the front door frame, into which the old lady had nailed a lock of my hair moulded in a ball of wax. That was the power of her healing and it stayed with me. Needless to say, I have never experienced that illness again since.

Writing this book, I feel a touch of fear, of apprehension, but what prevails is the fiery desire to tell the story of the Crone, the witch, Baba Yaga, as I know her. She demands to be spoken about. She wants to be known. She came on the morning of the Full Moon in February and took possession of my awareness. She held on tight and I could not ignore the feeling or shake the energy off. I had to learn to listen harder and stay with the unknown. For an intuitive witch she was the one, who sees beyond what's possible. I had to own my intuitive magic once again.

I woke up with the sense of her in my skin, her words on my lips and her face close to mine. Her breath was cold, indescribable, terrifying, but I tried to hold my nerve and bow in reverence. She knows me too. I will have the rest of my life to get to know her. Unpredictable, scolding, enraged one minute and then contained to such a degree in the next minute that my whole body shakes in admiration. Changeable, transformative and full of value. To me she is a character that once she trusts you can do the work, always has your back; if she doesn't, she will not be interested.

Chapter 3

Experiencing Baba Yaga and Her Lessons

Connection through dreams

One of the ways that Baba Yaga may communicate with you is through dreams. It has always been my experience.

Dreams offer very rich material to us in terms of what we need to integrate, embrace, celebrate and learn about ourselves. Dreams are great tools in our quest for self-realisation and individuation. If one is fully conscious of dreams' potentialities, one will be welcomed into the rich world of symbols, which can ultimately lead us to the core of ourselves.

Journal entry

I had a dream this week, which strongly connected me to the "Crone" side of myself. I felt this incredible power deep inside my being and a sense of "anything is possible" in both terms – shadow and light, destroy and flourish, love and force, revenge and forgiveness, anger and surrender. The feelings that one wakes up with in the morning after a powerful dream cannot be made up. It is potent, it is there and it is leading us to where we are meant to be going in terms of manifesting our own qualities into our daily lives, decoding symbols and messages and making sense of what it is like to be us, to be fully conscious of the paradigms and realities we find ourselves in.

The dream sparked my strong resonance with Baba Yaga. It revealed my open connection with her qualities and the feeling of being attracted to her ways. I realised that she was becoming a strong part of me. I spent my day in contemplation of what it meant for me and, of course, messages became clear pointing me towards certain qualities that I had within me, which the Crone planted into my soul. It was also pointing towards my past wounds, which I suppressed and buried in the shadow. It told me it was time I looked at this fully. It is inevitable and I always knew it would surface and what a wonderful way to face it. The material I have been avoiding is rich with valuable lessons and ultimately seeking to help me become a fully integrated person. It's been long time coming and I am in love with the process of unfolding through *imagery and stirrings in my soul via the power of a deity so sacred.*

Connection through the Elements, symbols and emotions

2018 blog post about how I felt (connected to Baba Yaga)

With hair smelling of earth and aching leg muscles I feel like I can fly. The Air element is strongly present since calendar spring began. Identification with flying, birds and wings propels me into areas I would not have visited before or even considered. There is space, openness, possibilities and opportunities. Ultimately freedom. Elemental change has been quite sudden and quick this year just as one day we had snow and the next all the flowers were out. From Water I stepped into Air, or rather flew into it.

My pace changed from the gentle quietness of winter to a very busy mind full of ideas. My views expanded hugely. I didn't just begin to step outside my comfort zone and think outside the box I threw the box away. I also experienced my clients having breakthroughs in their process one after another. There was an opening of some sort, which again invited us all, it seems, into being something different. This all feels like a big change overnight.

What I am working on now is bringing myself back into balance and what is needed is Earth. So, I walk a lot. I wash my hair (crown chakra) with clay and mud and exercise my body so I can feel every muscle and joint to connect me to the physical. It is grounding. On my walk today I encountered a heron that I often see and even though it was a bird, a lot of them in my awareness right now, heron is a wise old Crone, who warns against haste and too much

21

speed. I hear her and I slow down standing next to the bird.

What I notice most of all is lack of fear. Courage is all around me. I feel like I can fly and not just that, but I also know how to. I am in touch with my skills and my inner wisdom more than ever and what also comes in strongly is a trust, which overrides doubt every day. It feels incredible and liberating to a point of "jumping" off the cliff and being ok. As many doors remain closed or get shut in my face, I find my 'wings' grow bigger. I find my way; I manoeuvre life and people with greater confidence and skill. I think things through and I am able to step away when I feel I have overdone it. Too much thinking is never good, hence bringing in balancing Elements is important to keep the overall effect positive and yourself intact and healthy.

I am enjoying my "flight" so far and I am excited to see what else this spring brings with it. In the next couple of weeks we will have Ostara and nature will burst into a blooming picture of glory. I am ready!

Baba Yaga is not into answering questions easily, however, if it is the right time and the right question, she might give you a hint. The rest is up to you. I have been experimenting with asking her questions lately and what I discovered was that she would appear whenever I needed to ask something, before I even knew it, and so her presence would alert me to an area of attention. I find this to be an incredibly humbling experience that fills me with gratitude.

Another way in which the questions and answers exchange might manifest is through me asking something (it needs to be to the point and concise) and there will either be silence, which always means I didn't ask the question right, or that I already know the answer or there will be a symbol/image/one word only that comes through and it is my job to interpret it. I think many other practitioners in the field of nature spirituality, especially those, who work with deities collaboratively would agree with this or might have experienced it in the same way.

Other signs of her presence might be a sensing/feeling of a particular energy. I feel it as an elder presence, someone, who holds knowledge in their body. My body responds to that. Remember, unlike some other deities she requires much preparation before you can have this sort of questioning relationship: it is the work of an apprenticeship with many levels to it (see Chapters 9, 10, 11 for further details on apprenticeship). You are not so much called or able to call upon her: she will either be present or she will not. In this sense, she embodies intuition for me: either present or not; not to be summoned; never preparatory or extensively wordy, but concise, to the point, and liable to show up at any moment.

There is nothing more precious to her than privacy. Her boundaries of high gates made of bones are a great example of how private she is. It is a primal/deathly symbol of "no one shall pass and if one does who knows if they return." Threatening and forewarning. She is very particular about it, so to be invited into her abode is a privilege and, therefore, the last stage of her apprenticeship. She teaches boundaries like no other. It has a great value for us all, as we have all experienced our boundaries being crossed over and over with detrimental effects on our lives and psyches.

I also see her as bird, a heron, in particular; aloof, standing and watching from a distance. I am always enchanted by their presence and, as mentioned in my journal entry above, see it as a message. This is my experience in this land that I live in. Herons come to the field beyond my garden after heavy rain. They like water. I take it as her keeping an eye on things, so to speak, and asking me to dig deeper, to ask again. Sometimes there is more than one heron and that is a wonderful sight, often three, which I think of as her manifesting as the Triple Goddess and in that way sending a message out into the world and to me. It is always a good feeling; a reassurance of the connection that is there. I feel comforted and in awe.

In the forest of Siberia, it would be a cuckoo, for sure, teasing us with a call, but rarely seen. This illusive and enigmatic being of the bird world, which do unusual things when it comes to breeding and mating, as well as staying in one place. That is, to me, the beauty of it; knowing that something is there, but not seeing it in plain view. It keeps you in a state of enchantment and magic. I believe any relationship with a deity should contain those elements. Sometimes when the weather changes suddenly, especially the wind, I feel her too in that flight in the clouds. She masters the Air as she does the Earth. When skies are grey with a threat of rain, she likes to fly free and I feel her then.

In my creative projects and writing, in particular, she manifests like a 'muse'. She needs you to be willing to get to work, to attend to a project with complete focus and attention. You must be willing to show up, and then she shows up as well to assist with her presence.

One day at the beginning of this year when I felt she was near in her essence I found that memories and images of her started to form. At that time, I commissioned a painting of her. I began setting up an altar for her experimenting with different offerings, and started researching and reading. I began to incorporate what knowledge I already had of her and my thoughts on that knowledge. I opened up discussion with those who knew her as well as I did culturally and historically. One such person was my father, who did the painting, which is on the cover of this book. I love how it turned out, very true to what I would have portrayed. You can look at it for a long time, which is something I have done frequently since it was gifted to me. I delighted in how she was captured, finding various angles in her aged lines and expression. She is smiling through her eyes. Yes, in my experience I have witnessed her smiling a few times.

I slowly began to discover what she liked and didn't like and certain resonance within me made me feel closer to her.

She didn't like cut flowers in a vase, for example. Not long prior to realising that I developed an aversion to cut or bought flowers first struggling with picking them in the wild and with then paying for them in a shop. Some things do not belong in a vase. Her massage was clear "leave it alone and enjoy while it is wild". This message was one about preserving simplicity and natural beauty and leaving things alone without altering their raw form. So, the altar ended up being very simple, almost bare, but energetically it felt powerful and alive.

Chapter 4

The Three Horsemen and the Masculine

To me, Baba Yaga's Three Horsemen (her companions around her dwelling) represent an archetype of the sacred masculine, in service to the sacred feminine/The Earth. They provide a framework, in which she can work in peace, blossom in her gifts and feel safe in the process. Their energy is incredibly positive to me and to some extent I felt their presence before I encountered Baba Yaga herself, as and when I was working and exploring the sacred masculine's role in my life and spiritual experiences. It is they, who protect and watch over without interfering with her witchcraft. It is in parallel with the idea of the King being married to the Land and in that marriage both the feminine and masculine are equal and have defined roles in order to keep balance. The Horsemen are loyal and dependable, constant and reassuring. They are clear in their role and in the structure that they provide. Together, Baba Yaga and the Three Horsemen maintain just the right balance; the unity of deities and archetypal relational energies; a sacred marriage based on the understanding and honouring of one another. It is an aspect that I resonate with strongly in terms of my spiritual practice and my values in general.

Alchemically, her Three Horseman come in three colours: black, white and red. I feel they are very important as specific tools and stages of transformation. The following are alchemical terms for the stages the Three Horsemen may represent as I see it. For more information on the subject of alchemy, if of interest, please see further reading sources at the end of the book.

- *Negredo* stage represents black, the womb of darkness, black night, winter, rest, dream time.

- *Calcinatio* stage represents red Sun, midday, energetic peak, the burning time, inspiration and passion, summer time.
- *Solutio* stage represents white, day beginning, pure, new, spring, young energy.

The *Solutio* stage in alchemy signifies hope, melting and releasing. It has a soft, watery quality. I associate it with an opportunity to transform, to start anew. Have you ever woken up early in the morning and noticed the softness of it all, the quietness? That time of day when it is hard not to hope for the best and feel enthusiastic. It is that return to a Primal state, a perfect opportunity to start all over again.

The Three Horsemen as cycles of the day play a central role in terms of portraying the importance of change, impermanence and balance. Nothing stays the same and at each stage there is something to gain. There is a time and a place for all things and everything must change and eventually end. It is a circle as natural as the Earth in all its manifestations.

The Three Horsemen archetypes can be used in a spiritual practice and especially for creating an even closer bond and understanding with Baba Yaga through including the sacred masculine. I have always noticed the significance of cycles in general; be it a seasons' wheel of the year, seven days of the week, moon cycles or the cycles of each day (morning, midday and night). I have been aware of differences and subtleties in each and implemented each in terms of changing energies and what is best done when in relation to the activities that I engage with. In the Three Horsemen you can find another tool for self-awareness to bring about the most benefit to each day that we engage with. We can integrate these energies in our practice and life and start to relate to them so that we always feel in balance.

Chapter 5

Turning Fear into Fierceness

The most recognisable association with Baba Yaga is fear. Those, who grew up with fairy tales would hear a story of a profoundly scary creature that lives in the deep woods. She is not just to be feared from a distance, in your head, simply with a mention of her name, but to be avoided at all cost. That avoidance in the collective consciousness, culturally and historically, points towards staying away from all things dark, as the threat of death, destruction, disappearance and being eaten alive were all implanted into the psyches of those, who have heard the stories since childhood. Not only has it promoted a fear of the dark, as represented by the dark woods, but also of the "dangerous" feminine energy, which Baba Yaga embodies. If we look at works of literature or songs and poems, at every corner there is a warning to avoid going off the beaten path, which is known and has been done before, and veering into the woods. Death will surely await, and it often ends up that way for those who dared. Best not. The idea of a dangerous female that must be hidden from view, the thought of whom alone should instil fear, is not a new one. It has penetrated culture, history, literature and relationships for thousands of years. Patriarchal beliefs show up through Baba Yaga's representation as something incredibly ugly and, therefore, dangerous, but most of all through her associations of being evil, bad, murderous. No young woman or child should ever go near her, yet it is children she devours and young women, who seek her guidance the most.

When beginning to work with this deity if she approaches you in your life experience a programmed concept and a recognisable view of her might be triggered and as a result, an opportunity can be missed to see what she has for you in the way of a gift. Our unconscious fears are powerful and have been programmed through for so long that we forget that there is another side to this dark, powerful feminine. Fear can stop us in our tracks and we might turn away from her in an instant, but what if we didn't?

What is fear? Baba Yaga's most associated emotion when it comes to the human world. Fear is a block, a way of resisting. It can serve as a beneficial function of survival and that is natural, but is that all that it is? It can also be a sign that, perhaps, just maybe there is something beyond the fear that needs to be discovered and integrated into life. If we don't try and overcome it how do we know what can be? Many people like to be afraid or need to be afraid in order to take action and step out of the familiar.

Baba Yaga's apprenticeship has several levels and I go into each level in more details later on in the book. Overcoming your fears is possibly one of the first steps towards working with her. She wants to be seen, heard, and experienced, but that requires us to become fierce in our search for what is best for us. She wants to have her voice used in life and, I believe, that was part of my mission when she appeared last year asking for my attention. She wanted me to speak for her, through her and about her. Showing her that you dare is the first step to working with her and it is no easy task, but do we want easy?

You might start by identifying what fear is brought up by Baba Yaga's presence, and getting close to it. Do you fear your potential? Do you fear your burning feminine power? Do you fear the truth of what she might reveal to you? Then, perhaps, you can sit with it and see if you can transform it into a fierceness. If you fear your potential, what is it that is in you that is so scary?

Chapter 6

Baba Yaga and the Seasons

I first feel her through the flight of a raven. I have them visiting my garden every day and I feel kinship with them. Dark nights begin to creep in towards the end of October and amidst that darkness her visits become more frequent. It is the richest time of the year for me; creative and magical. The time that provides me with the best clarity of mind, the most luxurious depth of feeling and a very sharp focus of intention. I feel the excitement of creativity flowing through me and begin to manifest my goals and desires. Baba Yaga's whisperings make me feel supported and I brave my magic like in no other season. This time of year, I feel that we are true comrades, and through my sharpest tuning into myself and the world around me during this time she manifests as a solid and constant support in all of my endeavours.

The two significant points of coming together with the Goddess for me are during Samhain and Imbolc. I set up altars in her honour and wisdom and show gratitude for our alliance by offering her all her favourite things: skulls, bones, feathers, stones, beautiful tea china of blue and white (she loves her tea), apple incense, acorns, dry mushrooms and berries. Colours of dark orange, greens and browns provide a warm and welcoming atmosphere. During this time, which is also not far from my birthday, I begin to practice remembering. This is something in line with Baba Yaga's teachings and one of her sayings/mantras/reminders is "REMEMBER WHO YOU ARE". These words have become my mantra and whenever I feel a bit lost or confused, I always go back to these words to reset myself. I also spend my time in remembering my ancestors, times when I felt the most fulfilled and authentic, places I come from, my roots and my sorrows and I connect with my magic in an active way.

Journal entry: Samhain notes

The darkness is Baba Yaga's domain and her overall preference of dwelling. She favours dark and cold, autumn and winter. She is illusive yet her energy can be felt far and wide, when she chooses it to be that way. She is in charge of what she shows and what she is not willing to reveal. Recluse and hermit, she walks the edges of the woods before retreating into the darkest part of the psyche and nature. There she rests in peace and magic, undisturbed. She is not easy to draw out of her territory. Things have to be on her terms. She is highly discerning in what she does, particularly when it involves others; be it another spirit, deity, animal spirit or a human.

As Samhain is approaching, I am afraid less and less. She is near. She comes forward and alive in my awareness. The gap between Air and Earth elements within me lessens. This time of year, always creates a build-up of various energies and can feel 'too much'. We can become vulnerable and even lost, but throughout it all every time I feel that strong support that only the Goddess can provide. I am familiar with the part of myself that is deeply knowing, trusting and calm. It is the time for re-birth and transformation, often quite a big metamorphosis. I have been dreaming of a surge in my masculine energy, as well as of parts being "killed" off, but the most important vision this year is the one with Baba Yaga holding a huge egg of potential in her hands. She is guarding and protecting it for me while also smirking and laughing wickedly into the cold air of approaching winter and she tells me to trust, to rest and be open. She tells me "no" in a way only she can and I understand it well. What she means is to be patient and drop demands for answers, as they won't come when I am in a state of resistance or anxiety. One needs to relax into a state of trust and faith in order to receive. She also reassures as always that we all know what we need. All that is needed is for us to stop trying to get in a way of things flowing naturally.

I feel very exposed at the moment yet also allowing and not afraid. Baba Yaga always shows me how inner wisdom can be extracted from sitting quietly in full attention to yourself, in perseverance and looking for knowledge within ourselves. She holds all the wisdom of the world yet she would never give it away freely, instead she waits for the one willing to discover it within themselves. She is not withholding, she is protective and encouraging in a way that makes you want to achieve, to know more and pursue whatever feels right at the time. I often associate the training into her cronehood, as a martial arts practice (something that I undertook when younger and consider one of the best experiences of my life) where teachers focus on patience and intentional, slow movements and a dedication to knowledge and wisdom. There is no time for nonsense.

Following Samhain, I spend the glorious winter months in quiet contemplation, self-reflection and expression through more writing and walking in nature while I incubate more ideas ready to be birthed in spring. Then Imbolc arrives with the appearance of snowdrops, followed by crocuses. Baba Yaga comes again in preparation for her departure and a handover to the Maiden energy that begins to arrive. Brigit appears often during this time and my work with them both comes alive in a new way as I say goodbye to the darker months and welcome the season of rebirth.

Imbolc

Today is Imbolc. Celebration of light, poetry, creativity, home, feminine energy, first signs of spring. Nature is beautiful when the Earth is beginning to move around yet it is still sleepy and stretching covered with seasonal blankets. Imbolc is the festival that I FEEL most of all. It is a feeling more than anything else for me.

I saw the Crone and the Maiden today, both energies flowing through me interchanging and communicating with each other. I take on one and then the other as I begin my journey towards the woodland. I was called to visit a different place and I listen carefully to which direction I need to go. A small village comes to my awareness and fond memories come back to me of that place, which I used to really love every time I drove past, I wished I could live there. The wish came back today and the woods surrounding the village called me. Without hesitation I took off in that direction feeling rather mischievous and playful. Driving, I began to sing out loud some Celtic songs feeling very young within myself. Maiden energy very present.

My woodland walk this morning was full of energy. I felt quite overwhelmed by energies flooding in and I was unable to sit still and meditate. There were so many things trying to talk to me, birds, tress, Earth – very busy. Life is definitely coming back into the sacred woods. It is cold or fresh, as I like to call it, which is invigorating to all the senses. I am aware of how much I love the chill in the air and the wind on my face and in my hair. I take a few deep breaths and continue off the path deeper into the woods.

My grandmother comes to me first and I am instantly taken back to when I was a young lady growing up in Siberia taking walks in the woods in very cold mid-winter weather with razor sharp winds for company and frost on my eyelashes. I was taken into that space and time, as if it happened only yesterday. Not only did it connect me to my grandmother, who lived nearby, but to the fact that I have taken these walks whenever I need to connect to the Earth or connect to myself for a long time now. It is a beautiful synchronicity that these woods welcomed me with pine trees mirroring perfectly that time in the place I was born. Pines are very soft to me, they are strong, calm and gentle. I feel very much at peace with myself and protected when I am in the pine forest and, of course, the wonderful smell, which I love.

As I continue my "feminine" feeling increases and I walk into the "Army of Ladies" – whoa. This is the only description I can give this spot. It is strong, but vulnerable, a little scared and cautious and almost prepared to fight should anyone threaten its safety. I had never come across anything like this, and I had to stop for some time holding on to one of the Ladies to see what would come. As I stand still, I feel a bit uneasy with the rather over-protective sort of grip this place has on me and then the Sun, the masculine energy, comes in and its warmth brings reassurance and balance to the place. It makes me think just how necessary Elemental balance really is in our lives, in our surroundings/environment and how different a place may feel when one or more Elements are missing. It always makes me think of a desert, which is the most unpleasant landscape to my senses as it is so Elementally unbalanced to me. I find constant heat suffocating.

I literally felt the tree relaxing in my embrace and stretching towards the Sun calling on her sisters to do the same. A beautiful experience.

The Lady/Goddess archetype remains strong with me for the rest of my very "female/Goddess" walk and I am feeling very much again in my Maiden energy, but aware of the Crone not far behind. She appears irritated and grumpy one minute and the next she sends out an energy of protection and a sense of close relationship to the Maiden. The Crone watches over her, but she tolerates no foolishness, or not too much of it anyway. I feel, as I collect pine branches and cones and go off the path even more into hidden places in the depth of the pines, the Crone's steps getting heavier, as she tries to follow me with a grumpy sort of posture and annoyance in her voice. The next thing I know I am slapped in the face with a branch and ouch... On reflection it makes me laugh and embrace the Crone with her holding me tight. Oh, I love her wisdom, warmth and necessary harshness sometimes. She literally "slapped" me into action, into focusing on what I need to do, on "waking up" and going steady on the path guiding the Earth, as she continues to stir into growth. Oh, we laughed and laughed and left the woods together. The Crone handed over to the Maiden and the Wheel turns again.

2020 seasonal presentation

This year things have been different in terms of how she had presented seasonally for me. In addition to her coming forward with more messages and wanting me to do things, she stayed around for longer.

She stayed, as the darkness has been up high in the collective this year. She needed to observe and to hold a space for it and this year in particular she was here to stay till the end of May/ beginning of June. Many a night I heard her cackling, almost wagging her finger and covering her face. She remained silent throughout, but very present. I felt a benevolence in her presence. She was assisting in holding the space for the daily overwhelming darkness that existed for many. Usually I would not encounter her till late autumn once she hands over her reigns to the Maiden.

I only heard her say one thing during her prolonged stay this year and it was, "This is what being in fear of me did to you? This is what not allowing so many to show up and speak did to the world". With many possible meanings, there are lessons for all of us in her words; something to reflect on. One day she was simply gone once again, and the hot blanket of summer covered my senses the earth and tress, and the world in a fragrant air of flowers. I knew she journeyed back underground to incubate her wisdom and continue stirring her pot of revelations ready for later on. I continued to write her story in eager anticipation of the time when we would meet again.

Chapter 7

Correspondences in Other Cultures

Born in Siberia and having come from a Slavic culture originally, I landed on this Celtic ground nearly thirty years ago and it felt like this was truly meant to be. It felt like my second home, a place I was always destined to re-join in this lifetime. Since the beginning of my spiritual journey I remember yearning for a Crone deity of this place. I was in need of her presence, guidance and support. I researched and read, I walked and practiced and I travelled in the UK and that is when I came to Scotland. My life changed completely. With my deeply intimate, passionate and soulful connection to Scotland came a Celtic deity – the Cailleach (a divine hag, a creator deity, a weather deity and ancestor deity) and she stayed. Everything about her resonated deeply and I have found comfort in my relationship with her ever since. Her images began to appear around me, but it was her strong presence from the end of October all the way through to the end of March that I felt the most.

Overtime I have found and experienced parallels between the Cailleach in Celtic culture and Baba Yaga in Slavic culture. Both of them are connected to their land and both of those lands I have experienced on a deep personal level.

I believe there is a huge significance in places and in the deities that come with that land and its culture. These ancient archetypal figures are deeply rooted into the mythology and story of the land and people. They grow from us and through us and our roots in many ways dictate who we want to relate to and how. Through building links with energies and places we bring these deities to life. They pave the way for us unconsciously and consciously through our genetics and ancestral history in many ways and we, by honouring them and telling their stories, keen then alive. In this way we become custodians of their stories, their energies, the gifts that they offer and the spaces they hold. What a privilege, I think. From that connection a devotional practice can grow, which is a beautiful way to be in the world, to explore, to learn and to worship, if you like, something that is historically, culturally, mythologically and ecologically important. For introductory resources on other Goddesses I recommend you look at the *Pagan Portals Goddesses* series.

The following poem is centred around the idea of connecting to the land and its nature, which directly means connecting to all that it holds and represents, including deities, archetypes and the energies that live in its creation. Everything is connected.

In My Dreams You Visit Me
In my dreams you visit me like a deep soulful cry from within
I am away, yet close
You touch my senses as I sit in solitude in the forest near me
A woodland brook takes me straight to the expansive
    lochs of you bosom
You contain and penetrate the essence of me
I weep, I run, I stop and I listen to the call that links my
    soul to yours
My breathing holds its flow as I hear your name and
    suddenly I am transformed into the old Cailleach
    walking the hills and mountains with deer by her side
The smell of peat, bog, pine and vibrant heather feels like
Blood in my veins, warm and homely
The air in you is essential to my survival
My feet are deeply rooted in your landscape
My heart beats with every changing season

I wish to walk here till it is my time to have my bones
    Scattered amidst your beauty
(*Soul Land,* 2020, Natalia Clarke)

Chapter 8

Bones, Skulls and Skins Magic

Animals are a big part of my life and my spiritual practice, so it is only natural that I would use animal skulls, feathers and shells in my magic workings. Baba Yaga's magic is an Animal Magic and that is very clear when you look at the overall presentation of the Goddess. There are animals dead and living, old and young, gentle and fierce, surrounding her dwelling at all times. She lives in balance with them all using their skills and senses. She uses them to do her Elemental work, commune with the land and to create companionship in order to maintain balance. She is the creature of the forest, lakes and sky, in charge of all the Elements and in complete alignment with their qualities. It would make sense for her relationship with the animals to be natural. There is more to it, however, as things are not always what they seem with Baba Yaga. One portrayal of Baba Yaga as the Goddess; which is prominent throughout many writings is of death, gore, blood and bones. Her fence displays human and animal skulls. She is accused of murder and human sacrifice. However, it has not been my experience of her. I imagine, though, that there are many more secrets to her skills and practices that might never be revealed.

Working with Animal Magic is a directly relevant addition to any magic practice that focuses on working with Baba Yaga. She does favour those learners, who do not shy away from the natural order of things, for example, life and death, predation and sacrifice. In nature these things happen every day and one must be able to reconcile with it, as part of a life cycle, and as part of our psyche, which contains all sorts of materials, including inclinations we might not want to admit to.

My relationship with blood - seeing, witnessing it - is one

of honouring the cycles. It often comes in my dream as a sign of rebirth, a new phase and the energy of renewal. I welcome those dreams and find relief whenever they occur. I feel the same whenever I come in contact with animal bones and skulls. It is a part of life, a part of death and rebirth and something that needs to be acknowledged and honoured. Therefore, when Baba Yaga's visits became more frequent in my practice I naturally turned to that type of magic in order to connect to her wisdom and subsequently to bring my own wisdom to the forefront in my magical workings and spell crafting.

Animal bones, skulls and sometimes skins and feathers offer different ways of working magic or creating a ritual whatever you are called to do at the time. This type of work might or might not be linked to your working with spirit animals or your guides. Notice that it doesn't have to relate to that practice. For me, sometimes working with bones, skulls, or feathers is intentionally about relating to my spirit/power/totem animals and other times it is spontaneous and, in the moment, based on intuition. For example, whenever I come across an animal skull or a bone in the woods, an unusually shaped shell near a body of water or in it, or a feather under my feet, I see it as a message. I know the message through connecting to how I feel in that moment whenever things like that occur. It doesn't happen every day and finding something in nature, to me, is special. If I am called later on to do something else with an object I find, I do it. If not, I put it away until the time feels right. Being an intuitive practitioner, I always wait for an insight or a call to perform a ritual or craft a spell.

Animal Magic is protective for me and I mostly work with the deer and have a set of small antlers that I keep on my altar. This connects me to the realm of the forest and all that dwells in it, as well as, qualities of a deer archetype; purity, gentleness, majesty and sovereignty. Deer are sacred to me and they symbolise the tender heart, purity, divine energy and sensitive nature. Sometimes this energy is masculine and other times it is feminine depending on the time of year and type of work that I am doing. Lately, I seek to connect to Baba Yaga through the spirit of animal including my deer antlers in a way of honouring the deity and acknowledging the cycles of life and whatever else is present in me that I want her to know. She is the master of the animal world to me, in complete unity with it and protective of it. There is always a sense of the old Crone being present whenever animals are around: this is another way in which I feel her or can attempt to invoke her essence. Working with the deer energy also corresponds to Cailleach as the Goddess and protector of the deer. (see Chapter 5)

Animal objects like bones, skulls and feathers for me are also linked to the Elements, for example, the Air Element is associated with working with birds or their feathers. Another way that I experience Baba Yaga's energy is through heron or cuckoo feather magic. It is something that calls to me. Working with the Air Element always feels good to me: it is the ultimate Element of communication and communion. Recently through the Goddess being more present I discovered that she absolutely loves incense. It is something that is always on my altar whenever she is around. The association with her hut and smoke coming out of her chimney always brings me comfort and a sense of belonging, of being home. It is undeniable that she enjoys smoke of any kind, as it is her Air Element representation in a magical practice.

Her sense of smell is strong like a wolf or a dog and with reference to fairy tales she always smells a "Russian", which I interpret as smelling a "human being" – a smell she is repulsed by. There is a message in that too, hidden and covered up with a combination of no explanation and sarcasm. She can be very "testing" in terms of non-disclosure, but that is an invaluable lesson in itself to her apprentices. Just think about the role of oversharing, offering opinion unasked for while desperate to convince others of your truth, speaking or even shouting over people to be noticed and many more manifestations of the voice not being used correctly or not being used at all. Withholding can also trigger our experience of a mother being absent. There is a lot to consider here.

She is also a master of bringing things to fruition. If we think of the two Elements that she is closest to, the Air Element and the Earth Element, can we see some things? The Air Element is ideas-generating, a networking Element or a personality-type, which is always producing and thinking, (overthinking even when it is in a distorted form). Then we have the Earth Element, which is an Element of manifesting, of bedding down what is thought, putting things into practice and integrating. She knows both Elements well. With her sense of smell there is no sneaking up on her: only she can do that. She knows what's going on and is able to discern if it is of any use to her or not. Working with the Air Element (feather magic) and combining it with the primal work of the Earth element in bones, skins and skulls – is a powerful combination if you want to work with Baba Yaga.

Some of the intentions that you might set when working with skulls, bones, skins and feathers are:

- Honouring an ending to bring about a beginning.
- Honouring and communicating with ancestors.
- Obtaining wisdom.
- Releasing and cleansing.
- Creating "death" rituals during Samhain.

If you are interested in exploring the subject of Animal Magic, I provide some good and specific resources in the reference list at the end of the book. I would also encourage you to continue to listen and see with intention and focus whenever you are in your sacred space or on a mindful walk. Things might come to you in a way that you don't expect and from there will allow you to create your own magic spells and rituals for creating connection with Baba Yaga and what she is willing to reveal to you at that point.

Chapter 9

Mirror Magic

One practice that I find very helpful when working in alliance with Baba Yaga towards progressing in apprenticeship levels is working with mirrors. This is true self-repair and self-awareness work and it can be as simple or as complex as you wish it to be. There are no rules so be guided by your intuition. What is needed is careful listening for when the time is right and when a question is right. Mirror Magic is also the work of being with an aspect of yourself, *as an aspect of the Goddess*. It can be as simple as looking at yourself in the mirror and feeling through what you see, which can have all kinds of outcomes: it may take you on a journey or you might get inspired to create a ritual or, perhaps, you simply sit with yourself paying undivided attention to the aspect of yourself that needs to be seen the most at that time until you feel it is done.

Mirror Magic can also be done in a traditional way of working magically with mirrors. You might want to conjure a certain energy or send something into the universe to be neutralised and released. You can call upon Baba Yaga herself, if you dare, but remember – the time and the question must be right. It is all about reflecting inwards and outwards. You can use a special mirror, a blackened mirror, an antique mirror, and so forth; whatever you have on hand or, perhaps, were called to obtain specifically from somewhere.

Other types of Mirror Magic include:

- Scrying with a mirror.
- Using mirrors as amulets and charms.
- Moon reflection magic with a mirror.
- Working with mirror symbology in dreams.

- Invocation of a particular deity, energy, guide.

I include some reading material for those, who wants to know more in the Bibliography and Further reading section at the end of the book.

In Slavic tradition it is considered bad luck to look at yourself in a broken mirror or a mirror left behind by a person, who has passed away. I invite you to feel through these beliefs and views and see where you are with that. It might not produce any reaction in you or it might make complete sense to you confirmed by a strong feeling of knowing.

In Slavic history mirrors have always been objects of power and wealth, seen as items of luxury due to glass being very expensive at the time before Peter the Great in Russia. At one point it was forbidden for members of the clergy to own mirrors, and gazing in them was not permitted, or was limited to special occasions only. Vanity was considered a deadly sin. The whole idea of a human as a reflection of God was in circulation, and yet gazing upon yourself in that way was forbidden. These conditions go far back into the culture and history of Russia and other Eastern European countries. Isn't it interesting then that it is Mirror Magic that Baba Yaga wants to manifest her work through? She goes against the grain of what is traditionally acceptable and it is in that "taboo", like so many of her aspects that she rejoices. She is a rebel. I sometimes feel that she has waited for eternity to be seen, heard and worked with and this is why it was important that I wrote this book. The purpose and meaning of this project carries value in bringing forward something so old, so precious and wise, something that is ready to be discovered.

If you are interested in the history of mirrors in Russia or other cultures from the medieval to the modern day, I invite you to look into the subject further and draw your own conclusions from what history tells us and from how we, today, perform and work Mirror Magic. There are many books written on working with mirrors in magical practice and stories created overtime on the meaning of mirrors in all aspects of our lives. It includes seeing a "bigger" picture, beyond the glass. Mirrors have become a symbol and an archetype in themselves.

Chapter 10

Working with Baba Yaga

Now that my connection with the Goddess is developing, for which I am immensely grateful and having waited for a long time for that collaboration, I reflect on the times when I was actively searching for her. Reading these journal entries years later I can't help but see some parallels in what I say and how I present things: for example, I talk about "flying" while on a bike, just as Baba Yaga would fly through the woods in her mortar. I believe that even then my connection to the Goddess was stronger and closer than I thought at the time. She creeps up on you throughout life and accompanies you in a quiet presence, like a spirit animal or an angel's presence might do depending on your beliefs.

I sought similarities in something beyond myself, which up until that point my nature-based path had gifted me with. However, connecting to a deity, an archetype, or a Goddess evaded me. Baba Yaga was about to provide that for me. I just had to wait. Patience is something she values highly and often in being patient we remain in a state of silence and being with the unknown just as it should be. Patience, quietude, a slow and intentional way of being in acceptance of all there is - known or unknown - are all parts of her essence and of the lessons she was going to show me by participating in my life; often without me realising. A part of me has always known, however, the value in being approached by an energy so sacred. That is why my journey towards knowing it consciously and being able to introduce myself formally to her or rather offer my services to her and have offered to me in a collaboration, is important. The journal entries below show my progression in self-awareness and insights that had been occurring prior to meeting the Goddess. I refer to my awareness of what I consider her Celtic counterpart Cailleach (see Chapter 5), which, I believe, was important as preparation for her manifesting more fully in my experience.

From my journal/experience (2015)

When I go on a bike ride, I am instantly called to connect with all the Elements around me, so I "fly" through the woods on my "horse", by the water, up and down the hill in the cool morning air.

Most of my musings come to me either on my mindful walks or my bike rides and today's topics were words and symbols. I have been using the word "witch" recently more often than before. I really like it. There is energy in every word that we utter, in the tone that we use and the feeling that follows. The word derives from the Old English nouns Wicca "sorcerer, male witch" and Wicce "sorceress, female witch". The word also has some Old English and Germanic roots, which connects with the word we use today "hag", which is what I resonate with the most.

A hag to me is an old soul. It is not necessarily an old woman with white hair and crooked teeth, as one might imagine. It can be a woman of any age, even a child. To me it is more about her energetic, intuitive sense and her understanding of magical ways, a 'make-up' that makes her "old". The old energy is knowing and directive, feeling at ease with the knowledge of the deeper magic of the world and all the experiences around us. It has an ancestral flavour to it and such souls, I feel, have visited the Earth many times before.

Ever since I was a child my mother said I was "not of this world", which being an extremely sensitive soul I always took as her misunderstanding of me, a non-acceptance of some sort or even a threat. However, my "adult, old soul" side proceeded in the way that I knew was right for me and that wisdom later on allowed me an understanding of what my mother meant and her "wonder" of me. She also always said and still does that she never worries about me, she knows that I know what to do, when to do it, how to do it and that it will get done whatever it is I set my mind on. That is the wise part of me that we all have, for some it is more prominent than others.

Even as a young woman I always felt older on the inside and I do believe that my being in a young physical body or my association with what a young body is never mattered to me. Physical beauty has always been of less importance to me in myself and in other. Seeing into people, connecting deeply always mattered more. To me true beauty lies in how people feel and express themselves and most importantly how I feel when I am around them. Resonance is key.

I have also experienced cravings for old age, I see a huge amount of freedom in being old. I guess this is something to observe as I walk into the middle point of my life. Another association and a part of my alignment with the "hag" is my huge attraction to the Baba Yaga archetype and the last quarter of the year. Samhain is the most exciting and "homely" time of the year for me and for her I dare say.

Magic is all about intention and manipulating energy towards the outcome that you seek or desire. Using words in the right way and with the vibration in alignment with your desired outcome is very important. I like writing my own spells, but also when I come across something written by someone else and it sounds "just right" for whatever work I have in mind, I will certainly use it.

As I fly on my "horse" through the woods fragrant with jasmine and elderflower I inhale the cool and pure morning air and I spread my wings like a bird flying into the new space of possibilities.

When I encounter water with yellow lilies poking their beautiful little heads from the deep, I become a frog jumping from one leaf to another with my feet touching the water, comforting and healing. I feel immense gratitude.

I become a ball of Fire with vibrant flames, fluent in the powerful language of the masculine, as I ride with force, drive and full focus. Exhilaration fills all my senses and the inner dragon delights in its power.

The old tree becomes my Earth and I hug the old oak and it hugs me back I feel enveloped into its warm bark protected and supported.

Post-Samhain 2017

The energy of stillness and quiet is present today post-Samhain and it is so soothing to the mind, body and spirit after the turbulence of the last couple of months, which were spent raw with an angry and sorrowful depression, the days filled with anxious hours and my heart feeling completely bereft of love. There were many points during the "die off" period when I thought there would be no relief from the twisting, reforming and restructuring of all that I call life. It truly feels like a process of rebirth this year.

There is no coincidence that it is my birthday in a few days and so I have a 'real' chance to be born again. My birthday this year also feels very significant, which is not something that comes up every year. This is truly a moment of transition for me. It carries a sense of some profound change, not simply a way of letting go off the old, but really stepping into a state of being new. The transformation this year is manifesting through the element of Water (the birth element of November) where healing plays a huge part. It is not the usual Fire regeneration and rebirth. What is occurring "post-death" is a state of cleansed and new straight out of the Earth womb. I am also being connected to the Moon in a very strong way and it is going to be a Full Moon on my birthday this year and I intend to engage with it, which, again, is new for me. I have some magical workings planned and one of the callings with this rebirth is to step into my power, to really feel it as I am being born into the new, and embrace exactly what I can do. It fills me with energy, which I can only describe as an excited knowing and quiet wisdom.

Today, on the 1st November I am also clearing out my altar to simplify the space. I want to allow that new and shiny energy to come in and settle. I crave simplicity in everything: bare, white, pure and light. It is a new beginning for me and I will be writing a dedication, devotional offering to the Goddess of wisdom and all life,

Cailleach, to ask her to take me into her cave of rebirth and guide me on this journey of connection to my new self and generating relationships going forward based on love, kindness, dignity and compassion.

Having given some example of my prep-work I would like to delve into my main story of working with Baba Yaga and what she has revealed to me as a result of our collaboration. She offered knowledge of what was needed in order to work with her and there is a lot of preparatory work that needs to be done: this journey, as many others, is a life-long one and you do not want it any other way. It is the beauty of progression and the growth in awareness, the relating, the knowledge and the heart-deep understanding of life, which is the ultimate purpose to it all. Be it a spiritual path, a simple life, an awakening, a state of enlightenment or simply living – whatever you might want to choose to call your life journey and whatever you seek to achieve and know, it is all yours and only yours. Treat it with respect, care and attention, as you would every part of yourself, of others and the world and many directions will become clear in front of you. For me Baba Yaga at this point in my life is instrumental in moving forward. I have progressed to a certain level and getting closer to experiencing her to the next level.

Remember, Baba Yaga is not interested in your stories, past wounding or any other "baggage", if you like. She makes this clear. In that sense she is not a healer, and I have never experienced her as one. She is a teacher, often a silent one with not many words on offer at all. She requires you to be highly attuned to energies by using your body and your emotions to know and understand messages. She needs to know your intuition is as sharp as it can be, on point and trusted by you fully. She wants to know if you are ready to go beyond all that you already know, and if you are able to see your own essence beyond the collective and personal conditioning and programming of the physical plain of experience. You have got to believe that you are worthy and to have done a lot of work on self-acceptance and self-worth already. These are things you must already know, questions you must have asked, before reaching the gate of Baba Yaga's dwelling.

The most important aspect of working with her is asking the right questions. It is not about receiving an answer. With her it is beyond the stereotypes or generalised wishes to obtain something, prove worthy or achieve a goal. This is simplified in fairy tales, the ones with heroes aiming to defeat someone and obtain something as a result. I have felt many times that she mocks that sort of path. It is linear and one-dimensional, as most hero's journeys are. Notice that women have always objected to that sort of linear existence whether they had been aware of it or not. It is outdated and leads nowhere other than to having to perform more conquests and continuing with more seeking, which has no end or satisfaction. There is never enough and it is never enough because there is never enough meaning in doing the same thing over and over. One has to do something different eventually. In one of the apprenticeship levels, she invites you to drop the familiar and create something anomaly-like, a different way, and a "going off the path" experience.

For Baba Yaga the apprenticeship into wisdom and intuition is not a journey of progression to the next and next and next, but instead is about pausing, stopping, may be going back several times and then moving forward again with a renewed learning. It is layered and once a layer has been explored it gets integrated into the whole and should more layers occur later on, (they always do), the process of integration expands more and more. The best description of this is a spiral, and at each layer of the spiral there is a deepening of your understanding. It is not all about challenges; it is about finding compassion along the way, showing to yourself, to others and the planet the multitude of qualities that exist within you and demonstrating that you are conscious and curious about it all. There is no end to it: this journey is a life-long commitment. Things will come around again and again in order for us to see further and feel deeper and experience our life differently as a result of each manifestation (see Chapter 4). The path of Baba Yaga is not individualistic, but unspools on a wider scale, the experience showing how and where in the world you fit and can use your qualities and skills for the purpose of understanding the wholeness of it all.

In the next chapter I outline each level, as I heard, saw and felt it. I make suggestions for practices, which I take from my own experience of what a collaboration with Baba Yaga requires. It is personal for everyone and there are no rules, however, I feel that there are basic similarities with these relationships, devotional practices and maintaining connections that I find other practitioners also experience.

Chapter 11

Baba Yaga's Apprenticeship

How well do you know nature and how you relate to it from within?

What does nature mean to you?

This is a big question and the right one to ask. Perhaps, you haven't thought about it before, but thinking is irrelevant here, as nature is vibrant, alive and pulsating and the best way to hear, see and witness her is through feeling. This is the first step. How do you feel when you are in or around nature? What places call to you and why? Try to write things down, formulate and attempt to answer the question of what nature IS to you? This can be a story, a poem, or any other form. Expressing something so vast and important is the first step to being aware of how connected or not you are to the natural wildness of the planet and to that wild place within yourself. It is a big one, so take your time.

Elemental awareness

Closely linked with all questions related to nature the following step is to break it down into the Elements, one by one, by tuning into particular places, landscapes, creatures, associations, positive and negative experiences. What are you drawn to the most? There is such freedom in these discoveries - I can vouch for that - and a beautiful content way of being with yourself through self-acknowledgement and naming things out loud for yourself and with yourself. Most of us have been in silence for a long time and this awareness has slipped through our fingers. We have dwelled in a state of numbness that might as well have signified the end. There is a whole world that opens up when you begin to work with each Element, each place, geographical area or with a whole landscape.

Seasonal balance and awareness

Are you aware of the seasons and is your life in any way in sync with the seasonal cycles? Does it mean anything to you? Start noticing in whatever way you choose. It doesn't have to be complex or mean anything at all at first, but trust that as it unfolds you will be able to see the changing world of seasons around you in a different way and be able to relate to it in your own special manner.

Psychological self-awareness

This may include:

- Coming to terms with your conditions and conditioning.
- Resolving your inner conflicts.
- Attending to your past wounds and integrating them (known as Shadow work).
- Reaching complete self-acceptance, love, respect and knowing 'your price'.
- Boundaries.

Psychological work is an investment and a commitment to yourself and the best thing you can ever do for yourself and subsequently for others. As your world changes so will the world around you. Psychological work allows you to come to a place of awareness, repair, resolution and integration of your wounds. This allows you to become free to move forward from the position of your present-self, the self that was always meant to be just so. It is a work of self-reclamation, of coming home back to yourself and being able to have an opportunity to self-actualise, to make all that you have ever dreamt of a reality. There is a real chance once we are 'put back together again' after a storm of human experience that has lead us all through tangles of conditions and programmes. The work of untangling yourself and going back to the 'original', so to speak, is the most important work you will ever do. Ways it will happen vary. Use your intuition here and zone in on areas that block or prevent you from progressing and, therefore, keep you in a loop of behavioural patterns that simply repeat themselves without resolving anything. Pin point a couple of those to start with and, perhaps, consider discussing it with someone you trust. It can be someone close to you, perhaps, a friend, or an impartial professional. You have a choice how you go about it. Feel through it and engage intuitively with making decisions and approaching choices.

Spiritual self-awareness

This will include:

- Understanding the existence of many realities.
- Re-enchanting yourself with life, the world and its inhabitants.

Imagine, just for one moment that there is more to this life than meets the eye. As you are reading this book, I suspect you might have thought this many times and have already acquired some knowledge and understanding of what it means to be aware of things "beyond" the personal, beyond what we see and experience. Re-enchanting your life means forming connective relationships with all things alive, plants, animals, rocks, trees, insects, water. This is based on a belief that the Earth is animate. It is alive, breathing and speaking to us at any given moment. Stepping into a possibility of communication with all that we come into contact with not only teaches us to relate on a deeper level to all things natural, but will reawaken within us a sense of "there is so much more". The number of things, ideas and possibilities that can spring from allowing other realities to be experienced is infinite. Curiosity will get you there.

Preparing for action

This can include:

- Developing curiosity and connecting with courage.
- Stepping off the path.
- Creating a "different way" of being, seeing and behaving to aid you in acting from the present moment.
- Start asking the right questions.
- Overcoming fear and preconceptions.

"Going off the path" as a principle when walking/thinking/ envisioning and manifesting has always intrigued and attracted me. Something in my wild nature has called for a different way of doing things for as long as I can remember. That innate instinct had been hidden from me, but never extinguished and in my spiritual practice and intuitive life I finally got a chance to practice it the way I always wanted.

Pay attention, however, to a rebellious side, the one without fear, you might say a naive one, as it can sometimes fail to consider all that might go wrong due to being unprepared. It is a careless, teenage-like, risk-taking side that dares to act regardless of the consequences. It is not the energy to use or rely upon at this level and if you feel that it is what is present within when you think you have reached this step; you must go back and revisit all the other stages above before you are ready for this.

When I arrived here, I felt like I was finally ready. I knew through connecting with the Elements and different landscapes that I could begin to do it. I finally felt safe, curious, respectful and being able to answer the call around me. This practice began with walking in forests, first, then mountains and then everywhere I felt the yearning to do so. I felt I began another level of training my intuition via pushing through obstacles to discover a bigger picture, harnessing the 'good' fear in unveiling another world beyond everything I have known so far. The practice of going 'off the path' offers all of that. I absolutely love it. It feels natural to me.

Every time I did this, I experienced something and as a result I got to know myself that little bit better. It has become a devotional practice for me and provided a deepening of my relationship with the natural world and with Baba Yaga.

Connection with nature runs through all of the levels of Baba Yaga's apprenticeship and every level that you get through you take all the material with you and enhance it further. Nature is her beating heart. It cannot be killed or manipulated and must remain the centre of your focus, as you initiate into this practice and progress through the levels. It is worth mentioning that "going off the path" practice can take many forms and I encourage you to listen to your intuition here. Some ways in which you might try this practice:

- A walk with observation of yourself and/or the natural world.
- A form of decoding symbols in every step that you take and what happens to you on the walk as a result of those observations.
- It can be a part of your shadow/integration work through noticing what you like and don't like mirrored by the natural world.
- Through noticing where you go and the places that you are drawn to.

The possibilities are endless and this is an exciting part of the process, but not an easy one. Whatever you decide to do or however you want to look at it you have got to be ready. You will know if you are ready and if it is the right time to move forward on your journey when Baba Yaga gets nearer and she will either appear or you will start seeking her more via senses, experiences, bigger questions, and so on. Here, intuition is the key again. Listen for that "yes" or "no" through how you feel when you decide to go off the path whether in a forest, in the mountains or swimming in a larger body of water than you are used to.

The journal entries below are examples of my early walks "off the path". There have been many more since and before. It has always been an illuminating experience no matter what happened, worked or didn't work on those journeys.

Crying your heart clean
Spring 2016

This week I am in North Wales surrounded by earth, sky and sea. Everything is in perfect harmony in nature yet on the inside there's turmoil.

I adore this land and its useful teachings and I ask for peace in my heart. I have climbed rocks and mountains, sat by the sea and today I am going into the woods.

The deeper into the woods you go the deeper the unfolding process.

The energy of the moss is one of the most delicious sensations I have ever experienced. It is my point of merging with the earth when I touch this soft moist manifestation of the earth spirit. It is what I experience as the high vibration of soil intelligence. It feels calm, comforting and cooling. I feel like I can eat and drink it, like I can become one with it. My body craves its essence.

Another sensation, which I discovered is wonderful to my soul is the cool "pockets" you can find in the woods where the air is very fresh and still and my whole body begins to vibrate. That feeling covers all my senses when I become aware of the energy rising from the bottom to the top and I become one with spirit. I went through the process which, if I wanted it, would have taken me deep into the darkness and then out high into the light again. I went further than I did before today yet I was not able to complete it, but maybe I wasn't meant to. I tend not to question when walks off the path are led by an intuitive voice. The overall message was again that through allowing dark emotions to be one can transcend them into a higher sensation of peace and joy. That was what I was working with. A relief or a release is always guaranteed. One always finds a way of feeling better even if it might not be clear what happens exactly. It can be subtle or profound. Interpretations can come in; symbols might come alive or it can just be a sensory and emotional experience of releasing whatever needs to go. This is my experience in nature.

The first stop was a fallen tree, which laid across a small forest waterfall. I sat on it reflecting on its symbolism in that moment. A bridge across emotions. I contemplated walking across the fallen tree and across the waterfall and in my mind, I sensed there was achievement to be had in taking on challenging situations full of emotions. I sat still acknowledging the metaphor of the natural setting in front of me.

I decided to continue walking and as I did tears followed. I cried while hugging a tree, which was gently comforting me. A striking thing appeared after – that tree was missing its top. It was half dead, one might say, yet it felt very much alive and no more or less part of the whole. I would describe it as a disabled being with the spirit very much alive and its softness was deeply touching. It held on to me as I acknowledged its endurance.

The woods kept pulling me in deeper and deeper showing off its magnificent trails and labyrinth-like formations of emerald branches. The moss got thicker and greener under my feet. There was less light. I was walking further away from a track. The path got narrower and the silence descended with pockets of certain presence whether through a pure stream of water running underneath branches or gentle white light amidst deep darkness.

Suddenly I began to run and got tangled in the branches, stepped into mud, got wet and eventually decided to stop. The pull into the forest was strong, but I made a decision to turn around. The possibility of what might have laid ahead scared me a bit and felt in that moment in time that I was not ready to experience it. That's ok. We are in charge of what we are ready to face and where to stop. I went further into the process today than I did previously. It reminded me of a therapeutic set-up with a client. I am often a client and the woods my therapist. You take your client only as far as they are willing to go, one step at a time, one experience at a time, one process at a time.

I came back feeling lighter and calmer.

This example of "walking off the path" shows certain requirements with this work. A willingness and curiosity to self-discover via listening to intuition. Not all journeys are the same. Nothing is ever lost and there are always lessons to be learnt. Below is another example:

Discovering your purpose in nature; communicating with trees and Elements

September 2015
I feel dizzy and sense another call into the woods. I decided to go and practice tree communication. I am dizzy still and I know that there is a reason and purpose to the feeling, like something is trying to put me to sleep almost it feels as if there is veil just above my brow, which is hanging a bit too heavy.

Message from the woods

I left the house with a clear quartz in one pocket and my phone in another to be used as a camera, as I never know what I may encounter on my walks. I like to document through pictures and being able to make notes and write if and when I need to. There is always a story, a message, a purpose that comes to me when I am out in my woods.

I still feel dizzy and as I approach the woods I inhale deeply and oh, it is so good to be out. This morning I pulled a card, which said – "go outside..." Here I am walking towards my usual entrance point, but what I find is a blockage.

I am immediately diverted from entering the woods in my usual way and I continue forward. The next entrance I encounter is a clear opening into something I am about to find out. It is a gateway. It is a different way in, a new one.

I turn right instinctively and from that point decide consciously that I am going to walk wherever my senses take me. I walk through the thick greenness of the woods. It is peaceful and so fresh here. I come to a clearing, which looks unusual and I know this is where that something is, yet I am not ready, I continue walking intuitively and see my guardian tree at a distance. I thought about "him" recently when finding myself struggling with the lack of the masculine energy within, the lack of Fire. I remember turning right a minute ago and it makes sense again, as not only does the right side represent the expressive nature of the male, but I was also meant to see "him". That tree is a representative of a male parent to me, it is old and wise, holding and understanding. One glimpse of "him" and I know what he is saying. He affirms that my energy is available to me whenever I need to tap into it. I bow with thanks.

I come back into that clearing I first came to and find myself feeling even dizzier. I grab on to a tree (one of the two standing together with an opening in between) and my feet start to sink into the ground, like I am drowning and I struggle to stabilise myself. I also begin to feel cold and I want to hug myself for comfort. I pull away from there and walk to a tree on the other side and even though there is no hill to climb, I feel out of breathe, exhausted and I take a seat on its root. I begin to experience discomfort, fear, it doesn't feel right for me there either.

Then what I see is a circle.

In front of me there is a tree within a circle and I know it is THERE. I walk towards it and instantly all is well again. I feel warm, the tree feels warm, my head clears and my breathing returns to normal. I feel held, seen and loved. I look up and I take a picture of the tree looking up. It is done

I feel as if I want to run home, energy within my legs expands all of a sudden and I smile as I take my route back home. It is wonderful to know there are many doors that you can see and walk through wherever you are; how many paths you can take when in a forest.

My message from the woods was healing and balancing. Just as trees talk and heal me with their interaction, so should I aim to interact with the world with love, touch, flow and light, clean pure energy.

Meditation

I rushed home to meditate on the scene in the woods. I was called to do so in a particular way. I needed to be wrapped up warm, lying on the floor (my best meditating position) with frankincense incense burning in a dark room. It all happened so quickly. I did everything asked of me and went deeply into it very quickly. Here is what came – tears, lots of tears. I often cry in meditations and I have always wondered about that. I feel today I might have realised that what happens is my emotional body not only gets triggered, but my whole being is overwhelmed with messages and with the experiences I have in meditation, which are often very powerful. I used to get fearful once tears came and would not want to continue and would often leave, resisting the unknown. Not this time.

I saw my physical body on the path to the woods walking somewhat unstable. I was swaying from side to side and had a big grin on my face. I was drunk. As I turned into the woods and proceeded towards the entrance point, I fell over and started crawling on my hands and knees and that is when the tears came. I was crying in the mud, helpless and hopeless, unloved and unsupported. That image is very familiar to me and resonate with many wounds within, which I am familiar with. They have been looked at and understood and what I saw next was an affirmation of my ability to be healed and remain contained. Another "me", a split off part from the "drunk" side of me gently put me against a tree, wiped the tears and covered me with a soft white cloth to ensure that I was safe, comfortable and most of all knew I was loved.

I proceeded into the woods, turning right like before and coming up to the clearing. What I saw in front of me was a huge Fire in the middle of the circle, the tree in the middle was on Fire. My being felt sadness, but not despair, there was a clear hope of some resolution. I needed to save the tree. I jumped right into the Fire holding on to the tree tight and I cried with it, I screamed with it until my tears and my tight embrace of pure love extinguished the flames. The circle opened up and I sat on the ground holding on to the tree. It was saved. The Fire Element.

I then proceeded to the two trees on one side of the circle and I instantly got sucked into the ground, not just my feet, but the whole of me. I struggled to come up again and then remembered the way of surrendering. I stopped struggling and looking up I saw a branch extended to me as a helping hand. I was covered in mud, but grateful and with love intact in me. The Earth Element.

The next thing I saw was from the other side of an opening, which suddenly appeared from the root I sat on during the walk where I felt exhausted and fearful. I stood watching water flowing from the opening directly into the ashes of the burning tree, which was now not in flames, but had hot coals spread all around it. The Water Element.

I looked all around and then stood right outside the circle in the middle. I turned into a white spinning light, and stretching my arms to the sky I span and span. The Spirit.

I encountered the Elements in nature and witnessed the act of balancing them all from within. They are all connected as a whole, just like myself is whole with the spirit. I opened my eyes from the meditation and realised that tears were streaming down my face. I felt happy and grateful for the insight and experience into what my purpose was, which was "heal yourself, so you can help others". Embrace your inner power, all the resources are within and all is available in this universe. The purpose is to love and be loved to heal the world around.

The vision described below made me turn around again on my journey: I was told that I was not ready. I was sent home to do more work. It also asked me to revisit, reframe and rewrite what I thought the path was, but wasn't. It taught me to pay attention even more and to never take anything for granted. This can come through visions, creative ideas and imagery that can come at any given moment. At the time I wanted to "jump off" into the unknown thinking I was ready, yet the Goddess (presented as a Raven Queen here) knew different. The message was clear. It changed everything for me. The power of listening and sitting with an experience however painful can turn things around and set you on the right course.

Last night's vision
September 2019

Black creatures flew over the loch at dusk that planted in me a watchful anticipation. They had the bodies of herons, bat wings and a sense of ravens about them. They swirled beautifully over the water with their sharp-edged wings, circling in perfect harmony and then settled along the shore edge. The sky shone pink and grey and water sparked in the approaching darkness. I held my breath waiting for something else to come out of this picturesque scenario. Out of a flock of these bird-like creatures a leader seemed to appear and as it unfolded its elegant, perfectly structured wings it grew in size and I sensed its leadership. It did not feel malevolent or threatening although there was a sense of caution in what was about to come. The creature's movements were gentle and carefully placed. It was in no rush to reveal its message to me. I felt I had to really listen, but noticed resistance in my body straight away. What part of me was going to defy this creature's message? Was I crazy? I watched in awe. I could clearly see bright light seeping from under its black feathery cloak. It was well protected and hidden and there was more darkness than light. I felt a stab of sadness remaining mesmerised by this creature's beauty. It spoke:

"This is not the place for you, not yet, not now. Go towards the light, not the darkness and embrace all that your life has to offer. This is not the place, as it drags you into the land's wounds and you lose yourself. It is not what is meant for you, not at this point. Draw the light from within and move towards it. We are the guardians of the lake and there is darkness that is familiar to us, but it is not for you to dwell in, not yet. See your own light and take the cloak of what sorrows you off your shoulders. Do not come, do not wait, you are not one of us, not yet, may be not ever."

I suddenly became aware of the amount of light within myself and a huge part of me just dying to throw itself forward in its rejection. It made sense yet it didn't. Sadness entered me once more.

The queen bird took her slender body off the shore and into a graceful flight with her flock following in perfect formation over the lake. I didn't feel relief. I stood bereft watching them fly away still not quite in possession of the insight, resisting it with all I have. This is going to be a continuous struggle and part of me wants it that way. Sad, hopeless, in chains…

The time and, in my case, also the place have always got to be right before I can join in the next step of my apprenticeship, before the next encounter with her. I must be patient.

Stepping into Baba Yaga's home

Ego death

This last level has only been revealed to me partially. I am yet to intuit the way for me to progress to the next stage. I was shown that the way the last level is taken up will change according to a person's experience with all the other levels. This is something I am yet to find out. So far, I have come to the gate and engaged in conversation with her through asking the right questions and holding the right attitude to the work.

The fence around Baba Yaga's dwelling and the entrance gate are a symbol of death to yourself. You must leave all humanly/

earthly attachments behind. There are parallels here with the work of other great dark goddesses that require a sacrifice of "no turning back", the ultimate proof of your readiness to step into the unknown.

I undertook such journey once with another Goddess. There are some differences and some similarities. It is in participating and answering the call that you will be propelled towards discovering more. That time I was called to journey into the underworld. I knew exactly where I needed to be and when. At the time I felt stuck in my life and it was uncomfortable and when I heard the call of the underworld, I knew that descending into the dark places of my psyche that informed my life, was the only way to move forward. With the call to the underworld there isn't much choice offered. You just know you have to go. I knew that journeying down would allow clarity to be my parting gift on the way up. Going through various challenges I found myself stripping layers of my life and dropping the fear of losing attachments. I had to surrender what was most precious to me. I will never forget the terror and the lightness I felt on that journey all at the same time.

Initiation into the wisdom of the cauldron

During the last level of the apprenticeship into Baba Yaga's magic you will be invited inside the house, which is both a cauldron of wisdom, a resting place/coffin, and a burning fire oven of transformation. To have reached this stage you must be born again, so to speak and on the way to understanding yourself, others and the world to a degree that brings you complete peace, trust and acceptance. There is a big "but" here, however. Let us not forget that an important side to this Goddess is her trickster character. She tends to disrupt proceedings if she sees it fit. There might be an ultimate test that comes your way here. One never knows what is to come when it comes to Baba Yaga. That is for certain. When we knock on that door of her hut, we never know what we are going to get and if we are going to come out the other side. We won't know until we are ready to do it.

Compassion and kindness to all and everything

If you leave the place, you will know what matters to you, others and the world, as one. You will again become who you have always been, released from all that has been and with a road ahead that is clear and open for you to create. You will understand the main pillars of how the heart operates, the most important and only place where all lives and all is possible. It knows boundless kindness, compassion and love towards yourself, others and the planet. You will feel it in your body.

I am yet to journey here and it won't be once or twice, it might be several times throughout my lifetime and that is how it should be. So far, I have experienced glimpses of it and periods of what I describe in that last stage and there is nothing else like it. The feeling of coming home and being home within yourself is beautiful beyond words.

Chapter 12

Baba Yaga and The Elements

The storyteller in this Goddess had to be suppressed in order for the made-up story to be heard. Her familiar portrayal not only served the collective unconscious festering in the dark, it provided the silencing necessary for control and for directing the energy in one way only. However, Baba Yaga is and has always been the keeper of the secret story that now really needs to be told and be heard. I continue my attempt to tell it, as I hear and experience it in my spiritual practice and in the intuitive life that I choose to live.

Covered up by a wicked cackle or a dark silence, never revealing herself but existing in a capsule of what's been given to her, she has been patient beyond comprehension. Like a Selkie she has been given a different skin and way of being; given, not chosen. It is through us seeking her that she might take the form she had always meant to take. This is the profound lesson in how via seeking something it seeks you and through seeking you it gets found in the process. Deity work is a collaboration but trust must be earned as she, like many others, has suffered through the hands of the human collective imprisoned by the story forced upon her. But the truth burns within her and she has been waiting to join in with us in order to reveal something valuable to the world, how to live and what to do.

Initiation into her apprenticeship firstly requires knowing the nature "out there" and how you relate it to your nature within (see Chapter 11). Working with the Elements is paramount, as Baba Yaga is the Elements. Nature is at the core of her being and she must see you being as one with it all the Elements for before you can even begin to contemplate entering her cave of wisdom, her woodland hut.

I would like to offer you a myth I wrote a few years back to demonstrate what is required, for the foundation of Baba Yaga's apprenticeship. This story was written after a trip to Scotland while visiting some caves up on the North coast.

The Greatest Gift of All

A man walked along a deserted beach when he came upon a cave. He had heard many stories told that the greatest gift of all lay inside it. With confidence he walked up to the cave's opening when suddenly there was a door that dropped shut right in front of him. The entrance was blocked and on its stone a face appeared. It looked like an ancient being, a female with long silver hair, crooked teeth and eyes as dark as the darkest night. Her voice was deep and otherworldly. She spoke.

"To gain entry to the cave you must have the wisdom of the sea, land and sky", and it disappeared. The man stood confused. "What does it mean? I don't like water, woods scare me and flying is impossible," he pondered on what the face said.

The face appears once more, "What you see as obstacles is something that your mind puts in your way. You are out of touch with your body and emotions. Within you lie the treasures of courage, vision, curiosity and intuition. Go out into the world and once you obtain the wisdom of the sea, land and sky, you can enter the cave."

The man walked towards the ocean and sat down on the shore deep in thought. Suddenly a seal came up to the surface and addressed the startled man, "I feel myself breathe when I swim in the water. It is invigorating, freeing and soothing. Nothing feels out of balance. When I swim, I hold faith in my body's intelligence and I know it will carry me through opening up the sea world beyond. With breathing you can feel deep within your body, which is a precious vessel for your soul."

"My soul? How do I know I have one?"

"By breathing and feeling the water, as you glide through its

surface and down into its depths, by merging with the ocean as one and tuning into the feeling of being in the body, alive and flowing. You have not been present with yourself for a long time and lost touch with what it feels like to be free flowing with emotions."

"That sounds simple," the man thought. Walking into the sea he began to swim experiencing what the seal described to him. "I feel my soul," the man screamed in delight.

He came back to the shore when a bird flew above him. It landed nearby to tell him a story of its experience in the air and how when it surrendered to the wind and allowed it to carry it the bird's heart expanded in freedom and joy.

"We birds have skills and much experience in flying high and low, but without allowing and being one with the Elements the desire for control threatens to take over the wonderful feeling of freedom."

"What if I fall?" said the man.

"What if you don't?" answered the bird. "Fear, control and a lack of faith is what holds you back from feeling fully alive."

The man reflected on what the bird said and became overwhelmed by a feeling of wanting to fly with the wind and look over the world from above. In that moment a mole popped its head out from under the earth and began describing what it was like for him to be in touch with the soil he called home. "But it is dark, cold and wet underneath," the man quickly started to protest.

The mole said, "When you get accustomed to being in the dark you begin to see the light, a special kind of light, a light that feels homely, peaceful and glorious."

The man suddenly felt a deep sadness and loneliness for he had not experienced any of the things the animals talked about for a long time. And so, he decided to become each creature for a period of time to live through their experiences and learn to breathe, feel, surrender and become comfortable in the dark. He decided it was time he learnt the wisdom of the sea, land and sky. When he was done, he was transformed.

Many years had passed. The man undertook many more trials and challenges in order to find the wisdom that the face on the cave spoke about. And when one day he was passing by the cave again the entrance was wide open for him to walk through. There was a bright light streaming from within. The man recognised it as that special kind of light the mole had told him about many years before.

There was a creature inside sitting against a beautiful lush tree with birds singing all around and water running off the rocks as clear as crystal and things grew in splendour of all colours. The creature looked like an old woman one minute and the next as a young woman with a small child playing at her feet. The creature smiled warmly at the man and said, "Welcome to your inner self. You have come far by learning the wisdom of the sea, land and sky. The greatest gift of all is your own inner beauty and wisdom. You are home now."

The man cried tears of joy and his heart filled up with love and gratitude. He felt in a state of belonging with everything and everyone. He felt whole.

Baba Yaga continues her work with me through insisting on a different story. She wants me to re-tell it and she wants to witness it. How does one do it? Through accessing feelings and following intuition. For me it happened through merging with the central element of Baba Yaga – the Earth element. Here I tell you a story of when I became as one with it and she was there to see it.

May 2019

There's a place in North Wales where the forest is like no other. Gentle yet imposing, soothing yet dark. I noticed the place being in perfect ambivalence, yet feeling the most natural. It never fails to stir the soul within me. Air so fresh that it speaks of the deepest, most nourishing sturdiness and wisdom. It compares only to the most delightful embrace where I bury myself utterly in bliss. Forest-

merging, as I like to call it, is by far my favourite spiritual and earthly experience where my body comes alive completely in tune with my soul and I feel at home like nowhere else.

One such experience earlier this spring reaffirmed my love for the forest yet again and spoke to me loudly of a place of belonging. As I walked deeper into the pine kingdom covered in emerald moss, I felt myself coming alive in every cell of my body. Both my skin and soul screamed for exposure, immersion into what I can only describe as the light of spirit, ancient and completely perfect.

Its welcoming voice whooshed through tree tops roaring me into its body and I became as one with it. Stripping layer after layer till bearing all I gently rested on its moist floor never wanting to be anywhere else ever again. Complete bliss enveloped my senses and pure peace entered my soul. I wanted to stay in that glorious house for eternity. Such feeling is rarely replicated in life. Like a mother the earth licked my exposed feet with soft caresses and I felt myself melting into the ground. It took a while to awake myself into the world again and the sorrow of separation entered me as I left the forest.

The Earth Goddess, Baba Yaga, was there, up on a branch wrapped up in her black shiny wings, observing me quietly. She was the witness to my work and to my bliss of the physical and spiritual and, I believe, she might have even smiled a little.

Chapter 13

Baba Yaga and Her Relevance Today

Baba Yaga is more relevant today than ever before to people of any gender. We are all looking for the same things, such as, strong belonging and connections; self-knowing; a level of comfort with ourselves in our bodies and voices. We want to grow and be challenged and no matter how unconscious our intentions might be, that yearning for something else in all of us is prevalent today more than ever. Who is better to guide us than an archetype that knows all, is afraid of nothing and is in complete and utter control of and at peace with herself, in ultimate balance?

We want a vision of progression that centres the knowledge that we can all have a voice regardless of others' perceptions of us. We seek permission from something bigger that is also within us that it is ok to go about things in a way unique to us. It is important to us all to be taken seriously, just as deities expect us to be serious in our relationships with them. Working with Baba Yaga will be out of the question if she is not seen as living and breathing energy that means business in the most raw and authentic way. We, as humans, want to bring a message into the open, as deities do, that it is not all sweetness and light, but that danger, risks and ambiguity are present and necessary. We want to be tested and to feel empowered with examples of figures, who are not to be messed with. We need her today, as we seek:

- Balance.
- Roots and belonging in the nature of our origin, with others and the world at large.
- Reclamation of our earth-centred heritage.

- Challenges that lead to big changes.
- Expression of our unique ways of being.
- A voice that had been lost.

Is she relevant today? Oh yes, more than ever. A powerful, strong, fierce guardian female archetype that shapes the world, knows nature intimately and captures our imagination amidst the crises that we face. To be authentic and fierce is immensely appealing today. We yearn for expression and the healing of both our wounds and the land and who is better to show the way than this all knowing energy? The way she offers knowledge can be a life-long journey. The whole point of devoting your practice to a deity like this is to learn, to have questions asked and answered, to transform in one way or another, to move through and towards something bigger, something wiser and to continue contributing to the world in ways that are unique and sacred to us. She is relevant at any stage of life and progression.

I have always been drawn to older humans and non-humans and excited about getting old myself, as the years go by. I see this time of life, as the right point of contact between myself and the Goddess, for which I am grateful. She is more relevant to me now than ever before. I love working with older clients in my practice, for example, and I find their life journeys fascinating. I am interested in stories, narratives, life battles and wins and human and non-human spirit. I fall into a space of awe when in the presence of an aged being, be it an animal, human or a tree. It emanates timelessness, something or someone that has embraced life fully and most importantly found the answers and accepted their life experience for what it is.

I believe darkness assists the light, as it is through diving deep in that we emerge reborn. Baba Yaga is called upon and many other Dark Goddesses when the wisdom of their domain of darkness offers a perspective of balance, of knowing what to do and how to shift it. They are alchemists, who know the process of turning matter into gold from the inside out. They personify it with their abilities to shift and work through obstacles using various tools; be it words, weapons, magic or shapeshifting. You can also seek to find the right tools for you in order to continue healing and creating.

Does she feel some of the issues that we face today? More than feeling it she lives it every day, but so do we and in that witnessing we stand as one. Can we learn from her? Can we decide to take action into creating a different world for ourselves, others and the planet? Can we see the way she sees or will our vision remain one-sided? Can we take a flight like a raven to oversee the true devastation of nature and the human psyche?

- Overcrowding on our mountains, do they hurt when feet stamp on their flesh?
- Over pollution of rivers with inevitable sewage spilt into it and the wild life poisoned. Does it cut off the flow of the Water Element?
- Cutting down trees to make space for houses, livestock, crops, i.e., profit-making in whatever way possible. Does she overlook the things that she knows do not matter?
- Poisoning the land with deliberate spraying knowing well the consequences of wild life disappearance and the depletion of soil quality.

Her story also covers the following areas and each of them can be explored through working with her. I would say that whatever area is meant for you the most and where attention needs to go, it will come forward and Baba Yaga will begin her whisperings into your ear.

- Beauty and age.
- Motherhood.

- Ways of relating to ourselves, others and the planet.
- Partnership with another.
- Male and female roles.

Chapter 14

Baba Yaga and Intuition

Baba Yaga's teachings on being led by intuition is the ultimate requirement to anything else that might follow in your psycho-spiritual work and magical practice with her. This runs through the whole of her being and intuition is at the centre of each stage of development and apprenticeship work into her magic. It almost goes without saying that intuition is what one should never abandon. Intuition is that Old Hag within each of us and Baba Yaga invites us all to see it as a new energy, a new way to hear your inner voice through her and to understand that there is more than one way to be, see, hear and manifest. She's been wanting to say it for eternity and it is one of the most valuable affirmations I have heard in my practice.

By the time Baba Yaga showed herself to me through glimpses of awareness or a visitation in my dreams I had already been committed to living my life completely intuitively for many years. I believe that is partly why she was able to approach and ask me to join in alliance with her. She also knew I had been seeking her for a long time. Intuition is one thing that can connect the conscious and unconscious, the wounded and glorious as one in a complete knowing of what needs to be done. It is simply priceless.

Working with intuition is a journey of discovering your own voice. It is a gift you have always had and we all have, but learning to use it in your life to achieve "Heaven on Earth" way of being, one must be prepared. If you would like to know more about rediscovering intuition and working with it in your life, self-awareness journey and magical practice do read my book *Pagan Portals - Intuitive Magic Practice*, where I go into a lot more details on the subject of intuition.

Chapter 15

Baba Yaga and Motherhood

When working with Baba Yaga the subject of Mother/Motherhood has come forward and helped me to clarify some deep-seated issues and integrate certain aspects. It is not only closely linked with the idea of the inherent feminine gift of intuition, which comes through generational and ancestral blood lines, but it is also about integrating the "good" and the "bad" within a Mother archetype. In my experience, it is the later that many have found useful and it has also been a healing insight into myself.

Baba Yaga is the ultimate ambivalent energy, which either nurtures or destroys. She is a great example of the "non-perfect" and in her ambivalence she is authentic and real. She is both good and bad, dark and light, fair and punishing, furious and caring, empathic and demonising, controlling and supportive. In Psychodynamic theory in relation to a psychotherapy practice, there is material, which deals with the idea of a mother having a "bad" side, e.g., being rejecting, absent and punishing. She is only considered "good" when she is attentive and always present. To simplify and zone in on this valuable point: when an infant/child finally realises that a mother is always both good and bad, an important part of integration occurs in its development. The mother can be there one minute and the next she can be absent, but she remains strong in her love for a child. This position of integration is called "depressive". I always thought of that as a realistic description of that transition into a real view of how things are. In that "depressive" acceptance of a reality there is peace. The mother is both "good" and "bad" and that is how it should be. This can be applied to most things when viewing life in general, which helps acceptance to come in and release tensions like nothing else can.

There are as many examples of qualities in this Goddess, as there are realities and dimensions to things and beings, human and non-human. It is in that richness of hers that I have always found comfort. On one hand, it can be easy to get lost and swallowed up when insights start coming in, but another thing Baba Yaga is good at is slowing the pace down either by disappearing or by clearing a space. I have really appreciated her way of being in this process, which I relate to. She is complex, but also very simple in the way she chooses to exist.

When my work with motherhood was coming to a peak and my understanding and integration became easier, there she was saying "You are all right". She can be incredibly reassuring in her simple words that are infused with such wisdom that the full meaning is not always obvious straight away. Everything that she shares needs reflecting on before settling with it.

If you have struggled with the issues of integrating your birth mother or your own inner mother when birthing and mothering your own children, Baba Yaga is the one for you to work with. I wonder how it might manifest for you in your practice. In mine, she led me through difficult terrain with simple words and showed me both her sides while waiting for me to gain my own insights about what her words and actions meant (often these actions and words were very few and hardly noticeable). She stood with me in the shadows in quiet observation and that presence of heaviness and lightness all at the same time was more reassuring than I could tell you. It is quite unique to Baba Yaga to be both in many manifestations and I always feel it strongly. In those times she would always come in 'black'. It is my favourite colour and hers too, I believe. Her black cloak always covers her face with a few strands of white hair peeping through. It is silvery and bright, like the Moonlight. Sometimes she rides a black bull through forests and fields or becomes a mole under the ground. Often, she is a wolf sniffing. Her affinity is with the Earth, which is the ultimate Mother. She connected me to the Element in its most raw representation where vulnerability and solidity of being are as one. She showed how in trusting the ultimate mother, the Earth, anything is possible. And just as the good and bad mother acknowledges the existence of both, so too does the Earth.

The Earth Element is the strongest in Baba Yaga, as I have experienced it so far. "Black" to me symbolises a *Negredo* stage in the alchemical process; a stage of the beginning, a dark period, confused and chaotic often, but a place of potential yet to be discovered. It is the 'gold in the mud' place, hidden, covered, but where all the magic happens. It is both a birthing place like a womb, and a tomb, a resting place of the physical. I always experience Baba Yaga stronger during the darker part of the year, which is her domain. Other dark goddesses carry the same vibration and similarity of manifestation. That always feels unquestionably natural and resonates with the rhythms of my body, mind and heart when it is happening.

I invite you to call upon her (in the right way) if you seek healing and acceptance in the areas of motherhood.

Chapter 16

Baba Yaga and The Witch Archetype

What does it mean to be witch? Someone asked me this question the other day seeking an answer in a sentence or two. Immediately I felt that this question was very important for any woman to answer whether you identify as a witch or not. However, I felt the question to be so complex and multifaceted, and so private for many, it would not be possible to answer it in a sentence. Furthermore, it is something to be felt and lived rather than explained. It felt like a challenge worth taking on and I have since pondered on it some more and decided to try to put it concisely. After all, the question was asked and seen by me for a reason.

And so, to be a witch for me means to be an *authentic self*, first and foremost. A state of being that contains all the wisdom, intuition and magic within and to be in that; to be able to live with those magical tools and skills always present and manifesting.

Baba Yaga is a deity outside of norms and conditions, unashamed, authentically open and brutally honest. She is in complete acceptance of herself. She is wild, sexual and raw, animal-like and primal. All aspects of the feminine that have been suppressed for eternity.

In these times a witch within us all can play a powerful part in how we live our lives if we seek her guidance, her connection and collaboration. Whatever your age, gender or worldview the witch is rising once again and it is very much needed. We all have one in us and it is high time we engaged with her and asked for guidance. Do any of you feel that something is missing? Do any of you feel the lack of your urge for life? I know many people feel that quite a lot is missing and we struggle through life trying to catch and gather parts of ourselves we no longer even recognise.

She awaits for you to rediscover, repair, reclaim and reintegrate. However, breaking out of a shell of oppression is no mean feat; it is full of fear, guilt and shame. The way back to ourselves can be murky and treacherous. That's where working with Baba Yaga comes in. There is a lot to prepare for before one is able to knock on her door. She lives by the principles of protection and nourishment, and will devour and destroy when no longer needed, just like nature does. She is the ultimate representation of the whole.

The questions below are aimed to help spark that deeper knowing within you and are things worth thinking about.

1. What does it mean for you to be a witch?
2. What would it mean to you to connect with the ultimate witch – Baba Yaga?

As the Triple Goddess she encapsulates experiences from all ages and invites healing to all aspects of our feminine human nature. The Triple Goddess work offers an array of integrating potential whether it is your inner child that got lost along the way of your life, or your Maiden aspect that has been wounded or motherhood didn't happen or was traumatic and, perhaps, an illness or grief struck in the old age. She knows how to deal with it all.

She is the keeper of the fire of transformation and a guardian of the water wells sacred to the feminine. She is a shapeshifter turning into a bird to fly surveying her territory in order to protect her kin, animal and human alike. She is the Earth itself. She is all the Elements in their most balanced state. She knows sorrow and distortions, cruelty and compassion. Nothing does or will ever surprise her. She knows what birth and death are and circles through the year with a deep understanding of transitions and change. She is a protector, a listener, a comforter and nurturer to all, be it an animal, a child or her male counterpart.

That full picture of being that she represents is something to strive for. Overwhelming as she might be, so full of richness of being yet we can all embrace parts of her and learn as we go along. From a delightful playful carefree and curious child, she turns into a brave adolescent that is open to experiences and ready to offer their minds and body to the best learning experience, willing, enthusiastic and passionate. As a mother she is strong, knowing and faithful in every action she undertakes. She is purposeful, focused, and contained in her immense compassion and love, unwavering in her protection.

Baba Yaga is good to work with if one has motherhood questions or issues that lie unresolved or unconscious in connection to a Mother figure (See previous chapter 12). As a Crone she is as natural in her own body, mind and spirit and as balanced as the Earth itself. She arrived at a point of completion an eternity back and the richness of her wisdom and experience is boundless. She is the ultimate Earth Goddess and a powerful female archetype that, to me, feels like the only energy that is right and flows through me in such a natural, familiar way. When she engages with me and I respond I feel whole, joyful and utterly fulfilled.

She's not without struggles, but transformation and change are something her manifestation is all about. Her showing us the struggle is her way of teaching us to be open to learning through facing our fears, pain and suffering. Through suppression and rejection, she has had to fight her way back into our consciousness through the centuries, both quietly and publicly. Today she sits in her completion and is ready to be engaged with like never before. I believe she will continue visiting us all one by one till we rise up in our own understanding of ourselves as true keepers of the fire of transformation for this land. We can rely on ourselves to know what is right for us, our loved ones and the world at large. The aim is to become as wise as the Earth, as powerful and transformative as Baba Yaga.

Conclusion

At the heart of Baba Yaga's message is intuitive knowing and bringing your authentic self fully into life experience. She calls for you to stand in your power with courage and conviction, which allows you to go beyond what you know your earthly experiences to be and step into realms of cosmic understanding and your place in it. She wants you to remember who you are and always have been. Her plea is for you not to waste the light within, but to carry it forward. These are her messages to us all individually and to the world. For me it has been the deepest honour, a privilege, a humble, awe-inspiring and the most beautiful experience, so far, working with the energy of this powerful Earth Goddess.

I wish you every success and joy on your own special spiritual journey if you are called to work with Baba Yaga. I hope you are chosen and asked to step forward for this life-changing work with an important deity.

Here is my devotional:

The Wise One
What if I took a breath and I was there?
With eyes closed transported into the heart of you
Talk to me through the veins of my heart
Within the blue of my throat lies the truth of my devotion
Do you feel it?
In every second of my life-dance I step into your cauldron
   of wisdom
Teach me more
I am open to a multitude of your lessons seeping like
   nectar into all corners of my being
To be, to rest

To love and surrender
I want to keep on knowing the treasure that is you
(*Soul Land,* 2020, Natalia Clarke)

Bibliography and Further Reading

Afanasyev, A. (2013) *Russian Fairy Tales,* The Planet

Blackie, S. (2018) *Enchanted Life: Unlocking the Magic of the Everyday*, September Publishing

Blackie, S. (2019) *Foxfire, Wolfskin and other Stories of Shapeshifting Women*, September Publishing

Clarke, N. (2021) *Pagan Portals - Intuitive Magic Practice*, Moon Books

Clarke, N. (2020) *Soul Land: Nature, Scotland, Love – poems,* Matador

Edinger, E. F. (1991) *Anatomy of the Psyche, Alchemical Symbolism in Psychotherapy*, Open Court Publishing Company

Helvin, N. (2019) *Slavic Witchcraft Old World Conjuring Spells and Folklore,* Destiny Books

Johns, A. (2004) *Baba Yaga: The Ambiguous Mother and Witch of the Russian Folktale*, Peter Lang Publishing

Meredith, J. (2012) *Journey to the Dark Goddess*, Moon Books

Mueller, M. (2018) *Witch's Mirror, The Craft, Lore and Magick of the Looking Glass,* Llewellyn Publications

O'Grady, J. (2013) *Pagan Portals - God Speaking,* Moon Books

Patterson, R. (2016) *Pagan Portals – Cailleach,* Moon Books

Patterson, R. (2017) *Pagan Portals - Animal Magic; working with spirit animal guides*, Moon Books

Pinkola Estes, C. (2008) *Women, Who Run with the Wolves, Contacting the Power of the Wild Woman,* Rider

Telesco, P. (2003) *A Little Book of Mirror Magick, Meditations, Myths and Spells,* Crossing Press

About the Author

Natalia Clarke is a transpersonal psychotherapist, writer, nature lover and intuitive practitioner. Her interests lie in human psyche, transformation, nature spirituality, spiritual self-awareness, earth-based spiritual practice, Scotland and UK travel. She is a fiction, non-fiction and poetry writer with a passion for nature, emotions and magic. She writes about intuitive living, psycho-spiritual matters, intuitive magical practice, nature spirituality and soul relationship with the land.

MOON
BOOKS

PAGANISM & SHAMANISM

What is Paganism? A religion, a spirituality, an alternative belief
system, nature worship? You can find support for all these defini-
tions (and many more) in dictionaries, encyclopaedias, and text
books of religion, but subscribe to any one and the truth will evade
you. Above all Paganism is a creative pursuit, an encounter with
reality, an exploration of meaning and an expression of the soul.
Druids, Heathens, Wiccans and others, all contribute their insights
and literary riches to the Pagan tradition. Moon Books invites you
to begin or to deepen your own encounter, right here, right now.
If you have enjoyed this book, why not tell other readers by
posting a review on your preferred book site.

Recent bestsellers from Moon Books are:

Journey to the Dark Goddess
How to Return to Your Soul
Jane Meredith
Discover the powerful secrets of the Dark Goddess and
transform your depression, grief and pain into healing
and integration.
Paperback: 978-1-84694-677-6 ebook: 978-1-78099-223-5

Shamanic Reiki
Expanded Ways of Working with Universal Life Force Energy
Llyn Roberts, Robert Levy
Shamanism and Reiki are each powerful ways of healing; together,
their power multiplies. *Shamanic Reiki* introduces techniques to
help healers and Reiki practitioners tap ancient healing wisdom.
Paperback: 978-1-84694-037-8 ebook: 978-1-84694-650-9

Pagan Portals – The Awen Alone
Walking the Path of the Solitary Druid
Joanna van der Hoeven
An introductory guide for the solitary Druid, *The Awen Alone* will
accompany you as you explore, and seek out your own place
within the natural world.
Paperback: 978-1-78279-547-6 ebook: 978-1-78279-546-9

A Kitchen Witch's World of Magical Herbs & Plants
Rachel Patterson
A journey into the magical world of herbs and plants, filled with
magical uses, folklore, history and practical magic. By popular
writer, blogger and kitchen witch, Tansy Firedragon.
Paperback: 978-1-78279-621-3 ebook: 978-1-78279-620-6

Medicine for the Soul
The Complete Book of Shamanic Healing
Ross Heaven
All you will ever need to know about shamanic healing and how to become your own shaman...
Paperback: 978-1-78099-419-2 ebook: 978-1-78099-420-8

Shaman Pathways – The Druid Shaman
Exploring the Celtic Otherworld
Danu Forest
A practical guide to Celtic shamanism with exercises and techniques as well as traditional lore for exploring the Celtic Otherworld.
Paperback: 978-1-78099-615-8 ebook: 978-1-78099-616-5

Traditional Witchcraft for the Woods and Forests
A Witch's Guide to the Woodland with Guided Meditations and Pathworking
Mélusine Draco
A Witch's guide to walking alone in the woods, with guided meditations and pathworking.
Paperback: 978-1-84694-803-9 ebook: 978-1-84694-804-6

Naming the Goddess
Trevor Greenfield
Naming the Goddess is written by over eighty adherents and scholars of Goddess and Goddess Spirituality.
Paperback: 978-1-78279-476-9 ebook: 978-1-78279-475-2

Shapeshifting into Higher Consciousness
Heal and Transform Yourself and Our World with Ancient
Shamanic and Modern Methods
Llyn Roberts
Ancient and modern methods that you can use every day to
transform yourself and make a positive difference in the world.
Paperback: 978-1-84694-843-5 ebook: 978-1-84694-844-2

Readers of ebooks can buy or view any of these bestsellers by
clicking on the live link in the title. Most titles are published in
paperback and as an ebook. Paperbacks are available in traditional
bookshops. Both print and ebook formats are available online.

Find more titles and sign up to our readers' newsletter at
http://www.johnhuntpublishing.com/paganism
Follow us on Facebook at https://www.facebook.com/MoonBooks
and Twitter at https://twitter.com/MoonBooksJHP